PUBLIC INTEREST
in the
USE of PRIVATE LANDS

ENVIRONMENTAL REGENERATION SERIES

Edited by
William R. Eblen
Ruth A. Eblen

Other Volumes in the Series

John Cairns, Jr. and Ruth Patrick, Editors:
MANAGING WATER RESOURCES, 1986

Benjamin C. Dysart III and Marion Clawson, Editors:
MANAGING PUBLIC LANDS IN THE
PUBLIC INTEREST, 1988

PUBLIC INTEREST

in the
USE of PRIVATE LANDS

EDITED BY

BENJAMIN C. DYSART III

AND

MARION CLAWSON

ENVIRONMENTAL
REGENERATION SERIES

PRAEGER

New York
Westport, Connecticut
London

Library of Congress Cataloging-in-Publication Data

Public interest in the use of private lands / edited by Benjamin C.
   Dysart III and Marion Clawson.
      p.   cm.—(Environmental regeneration series)
  Bibliography: p.
  Includes index.
  Contents: Public interest in the use of private lands / Marion
Clawson and Benjamin C. Dysart III—Multi-media aspects of waste
management—Raymond C. Loehr—Effective toxics management /
David L. Morell—Biotechnology and thoroughbred agriculture /
Jack Doyle—Maintaining agricultural land as the petroleum era
passes / R. Neil Sampson—Agricultural land / Pierre Crosson—
Siting industrial facilities in the western United States—Joseph
B. Browder—Acid rain / John A. Thorner—Comprehensive planning
and environmental ethos—Evan C. Vlachos—Land use /
Norman A. Berg—Innovative process and inventive solutions /
Elizabeth Peelle.
  ISBN 0-275-92991-4 (alk. paper)
  1. Land use—Government policy—United States. 2. Land use—
Environmental aspects—United States. 3. Right of property—United
States. 4. Land use—Government policy. 5. Land use—Environmental
aspects. 6. Right of property.   I. Dysart, Benjamin C.
II. Clawson, Marion. III. Series.
HD205.P84   1989
333.73'15'0973—dc20   89–3913

Library of Congress Catalog Card Number: 89-3913
ISBN: 0-275-92991-4

First published in 1989

Praeger Publishers, One Madison Avenue, New York, NY 10010
A division of Greenwood Press, Inc.

Printed in the United States of America

The paper used in this book complies with the
Permanent Paper Standard issued by the National
Information Standards Organization (Z39.48-1984).

10 9 8 7 6 5 4 3 2 1

Contents

Series Foreword

Now and then in my dreams, I see a place where one might initiate and publicize programs to give the environment movement a positive constructive philosophy that would complement the present defensive attitude of environmental conservation and protection.

René Dubos, 1975

The René Dubos Center for Human Environments, a nonprofit education and research organization, was founded by the eminent scientist/humanist in 1975 to focus on the humanistic and social aspects of environmental problems. Whereas other organizations deal with the protection of the environment, the Dubos Center is primarily concerned with the interplay between human life and environmental situations. It complements the defensive policies of the environmental movement by emphasizing the creative aspects of human interventions into nature.

In 1981, Dr. Dubos convened an international conference to honor Lady Jackson, Barbara Ward, who died in May of 1981—for it was their plan to commemorate the 10th anniversary of the historic United Nations Conference on the Human Environment held in Stockholm in 1972. I had agreed, along with some 30 world leaders, to help him carry out their plan to assess the progress made in the first decade with a view to developing an action agenda for a more hopeful and positive future. It had been my great privilege, as Secretary-General of the Stockholm Conference, to introduce René Dubos and Barbara Ward and to enlist their cooperation in producing, with the support of some 100 other leaders from around the world, the book *Only One Earth*, which became the principal source of guidance and inspiration for that conference.

René Dubos died on February 20, 1982, his 81st birthday. Mrs. Dubos, his colleagues, and the conveners all agreed that the convocation, although it had to be delayed, should go on as a living memorial to René Dubos as well as to Barbara Ward—and as a means of ensuring that the work and mission of René Dubos would continue through the Center that he founded, which bears his name and which continues his work.

I was honored to be invited to serve as Chairman of The International Convocation for World Environmental Regeneration that took place in February 1983, at the Waldorf-Astoria in New York City.

On the last day of the conference, a special meeting was held at The Rockefeller University to develop the action agenda for the Dubos Center's forum program. It calls for constructive dialogue among diverse authorities with an emphasis on sharing strategies that have proven to be significant in dealing with specific issues within each of the following areas addressed at the International Convocation:

• Environment and Human Health
• Managing Water Resources
• Land and Human Settlements
• Science, Technology, and Human Values.

The practical purpose of The René Dubos Center's forum program is to acquire and integrate knowledge needed by the general public, not technical but rather focused on costs, benefits, and long-range consequences of the issues, and to help formulate policies for the resolution of environmental conflicts and for the creation of new environmental values.

The workshops at each forum emphasize constructive dialogue and evaluation of major issues and the definition of areas of agreement and disagreement among the participating authorities who create, enforce, and are affected by environmental legislation. Case histories of creative solutions are cited whenever possible.

One tangible product of the Dubos Forum Program is this series of Environmental Regeneration books. The first book on *Managing Water Resources*, edited by John Cairns, Jr., and Ruth Patrick, was based on the Dubos Forum of the same name. *Managing Public Lands in the Public Interest* and *Public Interest in the Use of Private Lands* are two volumes generated by the Dubos Forum on land management and edited by Benjamin C. Dysart, III and Marion Clawson. It is hoped that the process begun at each forum will be continued and enhanced by publishing the findings and opinions of scientists and policy makers from all sectors of our society. In this way, the ripple effect of these dialogues begun among a small group of authorities will suggest creative new solutions to the environmental problems facing the human community.

Maurice F. Strong

Acknowledgments

My distinguished co-editor, Marion Clawson, has written and edited so many books about land resources and its management over the last half century that he has probably acknowledged all or most of those who contributed to his successes. That is not the case with me.

With respect to land resources, I acknowledge three persons who shared their values and taught me to respect and appreciate the land, what grows on it, and the creatures found in the woodlands, wetlands, streams, and mountains: my father, my grandfather, and Maury Leftwich.

I also acknowledge the substantial support from the private sector that has made possible a great deal of my research. This has allowed me to think about, work on, and contribute to better understanding the linkages among land resources, people, institutions, and economic activity as well as how managers and resource professionals can make better-informed and more responsible trade-offs in the real world. Individuals who have been particularly helpful over the last 15 years are Jim Hendricks, John Garton, and top management at Duke Power.

Finally, I must acknowledge the 100 or so graduate students who have helped do most of my research and whose theses and dissertations have served to create, capture, and advance some exciting ideas important in better managing and protecting our land and related water resources.

Marion joins me in acknowledging our great indebtedness to my secretary, Patsy Phillips. Marion and I had the pleasure of editing, and Patsy did most of the work that caused the authors' initially fine chapters and our editing to become an even better manuscript. It is a tribute to her professional skill that she made our work—and that of all the authors—go so smoothly.

We would also like to thank Ada Louise Steirer for doing an excellent job in compiling the index for this book.

Ben Dysart

PUBLIC INTEREST
in the
USE of PRIVATE LANDS

1

Public Interest in the Use of Private Lands: An Overview

Marion Clawson and Benjamin C. Dysart III

ABSTRACT

Every person—of every age, both sexes, and all races—lives, works, plays, and otherwise uses land every day. Land supplies most of the food, most of the water, all the paper, all the minerals, and most of the beauty for each person. Land is basic to the individual, the community, the nation, and the world. Concern over land use is, therefore, proper and fitting. Most land, the great majority of it in the United States, is privately owned by individuals or corporations. This means, for example, that most of the energy is produced and distributed, most of the forest products and agricultural commodities are raised, most recreation takes place, most people live and work, most toxic wastes are stored or are being destroyed, and most of our goods are produced and services provided in, on, or from private lands. Because of this, it is very important to all individuals and interests not only how public lands are managed but also how the private lands of our nation are managed. Good stewardship and socially responsible resource-related trade-offs are at least as critical for our private lands as for the public lands.

Key Words: land use, private land, trade-offs, decision making, public interest, public controls, externalities, interrelationships, linkages, resource management, planning process.

DESIRE TO OWN LAND

The desire to own land is age-old. In every society and economy of the world, throughout the ages, people have wished to own land. This desire has not been realized by everyone in most—perhaps in all—

societies. Some persons and families have not been able to attain land-ownership, but they have nonetheless been land users in the basic ways stated earlier.

In the United States today, landownership, particularly as ownership of a dwelling and the land on which it rests, is still extremely important. Fortunately, far more than half of all families or individuals do own their residences, often with substantial mortgages. But it is perhaps less important to own land in the United States today than it once was in this country and as it is in most other countries of the world. That is, one can obtain the use of land by renting a residence, by buying the products of the farm and forest, and by otherwise getting to use land or its products without actually owning the land. Economic security and well-being, social standing, and political position in the United States today do not require actual ownership of land, although such ownership is normally advantageous for each of these objectives.

CONCEPTS OF LANDOWNERSHIP

Concepts of ownership, as applied to land, have changed over the past century in the United States. At one time, the landowner had virtually unlimited power to use or abuse the land as he or she chose. The notion of what sorts of activities constitute wise and proper use or irresponsible abuse has changed some with the times. Subject only to the law of nuisance—which was not very effective—the owner could make use of land as he or she chose without consideration for the effects on other persons.

"My home is my castle" was the dominant philosophy. The land-owner in the United States a hundred years ago typically owned from "the center of the earth to the zenith of the sky." The United States was one of the few countries where ownership of the surface of the land also conveyed ownership of the minerals within the land. This latter situation has been modified in practice more than most Americans realize, as titles to surface and subsurface have been divided between person and government or between different persons. The federal government, for instance, owns the minerals on more than 60 million acres of land, the titles to the surface of which are owned by individuals.

Over the past several decades, this concept of unlimited rights from private ownership of land has gradually been modified to a substantial degree by legislation, by court decisions, and by private attitudes and actions. Today, there is virtually no land in the United States where its use is not to some degree affected by public action. As a society, we have asserted a social interest in private land use. Social controls range from very strict or severe to very mild. At one extreme, society may totally prohibit some land use on some private lands; or, at the other extreme, it may offer some rather mild economic inducements to desired uses of private land. Society as a whole—frequently speaking through diverse interest groups on a local, regional, or national scale—is being heard and is increasingly influential in private land-use decisions.

The United States is not alone in the exercise by society of controls over private land use. Virtually every other country in the world also exercises such controls, and typically more controls and more severe ones in other countries than in the United States. The people of the world, working through their governments, have simply said that use of land is too important a matter to be entrusted entirely to the private market.

Bases for Social Controls over Private Land Use

Social controls over private land use may be justified on one or more of several bases, either explicitly or implicitly. First of all, safety and health of the populace or some significant part of it, or even of the landowner or land user alone, may be the basis for some social controls over land use. In the United States, we have building codes to prevent or reduce shoddy building that might endanger the health of the occupants of the structure, health codes to prevent or reduce unhealthy uses of land and structures, limitations on building in high-hazard areas such as flood plains and earthquake fault lines, and others. We simply assert—often more implicitly than explicitly—that society as a whole has an interest in the welfare of its citizens that can override the wishes of the private landowner.

A second basis for public controls over private land use lies in efficiency. The value, in the market or in use, of any property depends as much or more on the use of the surrounding properties as it does on anything that takes place on the particular parcel of land. The finest residence has little value in a slum, for instance; the classic case in the law texts is that of the slaughterhouse or the glue factory in the prime residential area. Today in the United States many residential areas of single-family homes resent the building of a condominium complex or an apartment house in the area or nearby. Efficiency considerations may limit development in some area to the capacity of the transportation system, or the sewer system, or some other public service.

A third general basis for social control over private land uses lies in equity. If most members of a community strive to maintain both the character and the quality of an area, shall some persons with sharply different concepts of structural style be allowed to use their land as they choose? If a real estate developer wishes to stretch and bend local zoning and set-back requirements—as well as the public bodies that are charged with overseeing them—to make some extra profit while offering no offsetting public benefit, should this be allowed, tolerated, or embraced in an established residential neighborhood? The majority may at times be unjust in its treatment of minorities—of all kinds, not merely racial—and yet the majority surely has some rights to protect its, the community's, and the neighborhood's interests against deviants.

Other basic considerations, or combinations of these three bases, may underlie specific social controls over private land use. Not infrequently, the true basis for social action will be clothed, if not concealed, in rhetoric that asserts other and socially more acceptable bases for action. A simple desire to protect property values in some area may be clothed in rhetoric about social values and the general public interest, for instance.

EXTERNALITIES

Basic to all these bases for social controls over private land use is the existence of externalities of various kinds. In an externality, one person or group makes the decision while another bears some of the costs (negative externalities) or gains some of the benefits (positive externalities). There is a disassociation of decision making and of costs or gains, at least to some degree.

The externality may be in physical effects, as when the soil erosion on one field or construction site results in silt or other materials in the stream, often far beyond the field or project boundary; or when a toxic chemical is used in one place, or discharged to the soil or water in one place, and its adverse effects are felt off the property, sometimes far away in time and/or space.

However, the externality may be primarily aesthetic. If my neighbors paint their house a garish shocking pink or cut their trees, my view may be impaired and the enjoyment of my home reduced. If, on the other hand, they develop a beautiful garden that I can see from my window, I have gained much from their action. In each case, they made the decision and I was substantially affected by the results of this decision. In the first example, they did not bear my considerable psychic costs; in the second example, I did not pay for my equally considerable psychic benefits.

The externality may be primarily economic. In most urban land-use situations, the value of a whole area is greater than the sum of its parts. For instance, a modern shopping mall as a whole is far more valuable than the sum of its single parts; each store—even competitors—adds to the value of every other store. In this example, the social controls may not be governmental but private, exerted through credit agencies and private developers but nonetheless effective on the individual land-owner. Likewise, in an attractive suburban area, it is the quality of each house that adds to the value of every other house. Controls over private land use may add measurably to the value of all properties.

Some externalities may involve the relationship between the individual land user and society as a whole. Two examples come to mind. If soil erosion ultimately reduces the capacity of the cropland to produce crops, then society as a whole has been severely affected by private actions. If the burning of all sorts of fossil fuels in motors or in power plants significantly affects global temperatures—the green-house effect—then future societies have been severely damaged by present-day actions of individuals.

FORMS OF PUBLIC CONTROL

Although the forms of public control over private land use are many and varied, they can be grouped into two general classes: direct and indirect.

There are several forms of direct control over private land use, especially in urban areas. They often take the form of zoning restrictions. These regulations may specify minimum front, side, and rear distances between structure and property lines; or they may set limits to the floor-to-area ratio or the height relative to the base or other similar restrictions. These are usually specified to maintain or enhance what have been determined to be desirable and socially beneficial characteristics of a community, area, or neighborhood.

There are building codes that specify how electric lines, water lines, sewer lines, and other features must be constructed; or they may specify building materials, or distance between wall studs, or any one of many other features of the structure. There are also health codes, which permit some activities and prohibit others within defined zones or types of structures.

In all of these—and in many other examples that might be cited—the public control is at least nominally complete and final. We say "nominally" because in many instances appeals are possible, and the initial decisions may be modified or overturned. Moreover, in what we consider a distressingly large number of instances, raw political power, blatant conflict of interest, or even outright bribes have been used to affect these public controls. These are flaws in the local implementation of a system, not necessary components of it.

Indirect controls may also take one of several forms. There is provision of public services such as water, sewer, electricity, telephone, and others that may be either public or private in management and financing. The way charges are levied for these services may also affect private land use. Among public services, transportation facilities—notably roads and their capacities—are often highly important. There are licenses and permits that must be granted by government agencies for private development—for example, the siting of electric power generating and transmission facilities. In addition to influencing the use of considerable private land, there are environmental mitigation and compensation provisions that may well influence the use of additional private lands associated with a particular project. There is also publicly financed andsponsored research, such as a good bit of environmental protection research and most agricultural research, which may very well have an indirect effect on much private land use.

Direct public subsidies to private landowners can be a powerful force affecting private land use. The payments to farmers to convert cropland into forests is one example of a direct federal subsidy that has substantially affected the use of millions of acres of land; but the conditions of private financing may be very important also. The developer of an office tract may find it impossible to get private financing unless he includes adequate parking for tenants or enough green park-like areas in his plans, for example.

The institutional tools for affecting or determining use of private land are many; new ones can and will be invented. Some will operate as desired, others may be less effective. Effective tools may implement public policies, but they are not enough, alone, to insure that such policies are wise. The evolution of such tools is necessary to help illuminate the hard—but necessary—trade-offs that regularly occur with respect to the use of our nation's private lands. In order for them to be as sound and socially acceptable as possible, these trade-offs must be much better informed by effective participation by all parties. There is much to be done in the way of developing and improving the decision support systems used by both the private sector and the public sector for decisions involving the use and management of private lands. These are needed first in developing an appropriate array of options and then in selecting one for implementation that will deserve the maximum degree of broad support.

INTERRELATIONS, LINKAGES, AND SYSTEM BOUNDARIES

The common element in virtually all the chapters in this volume is the same as that encountered in any critical environmental quality or resource-related dialogue today in our nation: interrelations or linkages or proper system boundary definition. We see this in the interrelations in land use (between one area or one use or one person and others, the linkages among all the components of resource systems, especially land)

and the absolute necessity of properly defining resource systems to be broader than traditionally defined for narrower technical manipulation. A number of these interrelations are made more explicit in the chapters; others are implicit but evident if one reads carefully.

For our various decision makers at all system levels and the numerous hard science, social science, and engineering disciplines to contribute to better decisions, we all must gain a much better appreciation of aspects well beyond our past comfort and competence zones. We believe the chapters that follow help in showing the way.

For instance, Crosson, Sampson, and Berg each examines—from his own point of view—the importance of cropland and of preserving its productive capacity for the future. In so doing, they are emphasizing the importance of this resource to society as a whole. They also consider the problems of soil erosion and other nonpoint-source pollutants to the farmers themselves and to neighbors or others downstream or downwind—and linkages to both the past and the future. Clearly, the problems of cropland use cannot be limited to those of today and of only the landowner or land user, but must include a much wider circle of concerns and players.

Similarly, Loehr, Morell, and Thorner consider the effects of various pollutants or chemicals, not only—and perhaps not primarily—on the person or organization originating the chemicals but upon a wider public. Both temporal and spatial effects—of pollutants and decisions pertaining to them—are presented. Again, interrelations among users of all sorts dominate their discussions.

Peelle relates one intensive and successful effort to mediate among interested and somewhat rival groups, in deciding how nuclear wastes might best be handled. Browder deals with the dramatic evolution in siting major private-sector facilities, and the very new conditions that exist for corporate decision makers dealing with public bodies and the various publics—conditions that can make it either harder or easier to produce winners, depending on whether the decision makers are or are not in step with society's preferences and priorities.

New technologies and new ways of thinking are also important. Doyle raises critical issues with respect to genetic engineering, an area that will surely be central to massive private-sector investment and land-use decisions affecting tremendous acreages in the United States in the near future. Vlachos discusses a host of philosophical questions involving land use in a most provocative manner.

It is not our intent in this introductory chapter to summarize, even briefly, the chapters in this book. They each consider some aspect of the general problem implied in the title of the book: how best to decide upon and effectuate the public interest in private lands. Each author developed his or her chapter within that general framework, but in a manner growing out of personal experiences and knowledge. Like all books consisting of chapters by several authors, this one is less tightly constructed than if it had been written by a single author; but it is also richer than any single author could have produced.

We urge the reader to read it all, and to see how every chapter is concerned—more or less explicitly—with this matter of interrelations among private lands, land uses, and land users and how each chapter contributes to an improved appreciation of the system components of land and other resources and human use and the linkages among them. We believe this can contribute to better understanding of complex issues and better informed decision making involving the responsible use of our nation's private lands.

2

Multi-Media Aspects of Waste Management

Raymond C. Loehr

ABSTRACT

The single-medium and single-problem focus of environmental control legislation and regulations has caused the multi-media aspects of waste management to receive less emphasis. As a result, there continues to be cross-media transfer of pollutants and reliance on linear rather than circular waste management approaches. To adequately control multi-media transfer of pollutants, especially those that involve land-based alternatives, the following are needed: (1) a deemphasis of the single-problem or single-medium regulatory approach, (2) a consistent multi-media emphasis that requires an evaluation of cross-media transfer of pollutants, (3) greater assessment of the waste assimilative capacity of the soil, (4) circular rather than linear waste management approaches, and (5) environmental criteria and limits for soil and groundwater.

Key Words: land treatment, municipal waste treatment, recycle/reuse, soil assimilative capacity, groundwater, sludge, regulations, tertiary treatment, technology-based standards, environmental criteria, *de minimis* values, risk assessment.

INTRODUCTION

Because of specific legislative mandates, pollution-control objectives have had a single-medium or single-problem emphasis. The cross-media transfers of pollutants that occur as these objectives are met are not trivial but have been a stepchild and of lesser concern.

It is appropriate that such aspects be discussed at a forum such as that of the Dubos Center, which has managing land use as the integrating topic. Land is increasingly used as a waste management alternative. Adequate understanding of the assimilative capacity of the soil is key to the proper use of the land for this purpose. Equally important are the environmental criteria or limits that should be used to assure that the land is not abused when it is used for waste management.

This chapter addresses important points that relate to the multi-media aspects of waste management and the use of land as a waste management alternative: (1) ecosystem waste assimilative capacity, (2) linear and circular waste management approaches, (3) legislation and regulations, (4) the differences between land treatment and land disposal, and (5) approaches to determine land-based environmental quality limits.

ECOSYSTEM WASTE ASSIMILATIVE CAPACITY

Each medium (air, water, and soil) has a specific capacity to assimilate some amount of residues that it receives without the occurrence of adverse impacts to human health and the environment. At times we have overloaded each medium. The results have included air pollution incidents, fish kills, contaminated groundwaters, salinity as a result of irrigation, and food chain transfer of chemicals. Many of these adverse impacts have been unintentional and caused by our imperfect understanding of the assimilative capacity of the air, water, and soil. Others have resulted from the continuing too-narrow focus on single-medium solutions to environmental problems and poor understanding of the multi-media transfer of contaminants.

The concept of an environmentally acceptable waste management assimilative capacity is not universally accepted (Cairns, 1986). Some scientists believe that any introduction of material from an anthropogenic source into a natural system will cause a change from the natural condition that can be deleterious. Others believe that natural systems have an assimilative capacity within which changes may occur that are not deleterious.

The debate should not focus on whether there is a media-related assimilative capacity that can be used for waste management. The focus should be on how to determine what the site-specific, regional, or global assimilative capacity for specific constituents is and the extent to which it can be used responsibly for waste management. The ability to make this judgment requires information on the degradation, immobilization, transformation, diffusion, bioaccumulation, transport, and fate of the constituents in the wastes and residues that must be managed.

There may be no "acceptable" assimilative capacity for some constituents, such as radioactive materials and some chemicals, that are extremely toxic or have adverse bioaccumulative impacts. For such materials, approaches such as permanent containment or ceasing production and use may well be more suitable from a public-policy standpoint to assure protection of human health and the environment.

Knowledge about ecosystem assimilative capacity and multi-media transfer of contaminants is critical to rational waste management policy and to the development of appropriate control technologies. It must be remembered that everything has to go someplace: there is no "away" into which residues can be placed or disposed. To have the benefits of a technological society while enjoying a high standard of living and a quality environment requires that a multi-media concept emerge as a component of a coherent national waste management policy. The following discussion examines the difficulties with current approaches and the options for change that can be considered.

LINEAR WASTE MANAGEMENT

Conventional water and waste management approaches are linear approaches. This is true irrespective of the medium being protected—that is, whether the approaches are for air pollution control, water pollution control, water treatment, or solid waste management. With almost all approaches, treatment steps are added on as needed to achieve the desired objective. Because of the focus on such specific pollution-control objectives, considerably less emphasis has been given to residues that may be produced and to cross-media transfers of contaminants that may occur as a result of the waste management approach selected.

Municipal wastewater treatment can illustrate these points. Before sewers were available, human wastes were an aesthetic and public health problem as cities expanded during the industrial revolution. As a partial solution to these problems, houses and commercial establishments began to be sewered; and an arterial system of drainage—ditches or closed sewers—was developed to transport the wastes from the areas of high population density to local receiving waters. This basically was the first step of linear wastewater management.

Additional problems arose when the discharged wastes exceeded the capacity of the local waters to assimilate the added wastes. Epidemics, such as those caused by cholera, as well as fish kills resulted. To cope with such problems, wastewater began to be treated to remove detrimental constituents and to achieve a quality of treated effluent that could be discharged without causing human health or environmental problems. Thus began the long succession of linear wastewater treatment processes that have been used to meet pollution control and water quality objectives for the last several generations.

Wastewater treatment systems are designed and operated to achieve certain goals: either specific effluent limitations for the outfall or water quality criteria for the receiving stream, lake, estuary, or coastal waters. These goals are to be met using primary, secondary, and advanced (or tertiary) treatment processes.

Primary treatment removes solids that are easily settled and that may cause excess wear or greater operational cost to subsequent processes. Secondary treatment processes are biological processes in which microorganisms degrade and stabilize organic constituents not removed by primary treatment. Primary and secondary treatment processes are generally considered to remove about 85 to 90 percent of the conventional pollutants or carbonaceous oxygen-demanding constituents— that is, biochemical oxygen demand (BOD) and suspended solids. The resultant secondary effluent usually is of sufficient quality to avoid fish kills or other obvious indications of surface water pollution if only conventional pollutants were in the waste stream entering the treatment facility. Because surface waters are used as public water supply sources, secondary effluent commonly is chlorinated before discharge to reduce the pathogen content.

Additional treatment—tertiary or advanced waste treatment processes, such as to remove nitrogen and phosphorus—can be needed in specific cases. Excess ammonia discharged in secondary effluent can (1) cause an oxygen demand in receiving waters as the ammonia is oxidized and (2) have an adverse effect on fish. Phosphorus can increase the growth of aquatic plant life and the eutrophication of lakes, reservoirs, bays, and estuaries. Chemical treatment for phosphorus removal is an advanced waste treatment process that is added to conventional or secondary treatment plants. An example of this need is in the drainage basins to the Great Lakes where the total phosphorus concentration in most treated municipal effluents is not supposed to exceed a concentration of 1.0 mg/l.

Industries contribute diverse organics and inorganics to municipal wastewaters; but because the secondary treatment processes are designed to remove conventional pollutants, only incidental removal of industrial organics and inorganics may occur. If additional removal of these constituents is needed to protect public health and the environment, processes such as carbon adsorption can be added as another tertiary treatment step.

Thus, when conventional secondary treatment processes are not adequate to meet specific effluent requirements, additional processes, such as chlorination to reduce the pathogen concentration, nitrification to oxidize ammonia nitrogen, chemical treatment to reduce phosphorus, and carbon adsorption to reduce potentially toxic industrial organics, may be needed. Fuhrman (1984) has provided a succinct summary of such water pollution control efforts.

The cross-media aspects and environmental quality implications of such linear approaches are not trivial. Two items illustrate this point: (1) volatilization of organics during secondary and other treatment processes and (2) sludge production and disposal.

Although secondary treatment processes are aerobic (i.e., take place in the presence of dissolved oxygen) and are designed to remove soluble organics by microbial degradation, there actually are several removal mechanisms that take place: microbial degradation, air-stripping and volatilization, and adsorption on the sludge. Other possible but minor mechanisms include hydrolysis and photolysis.

Air stripping and adsorption can be important removal mechanisms for organic compounds that may have high volatility or adsorb strongly to the microbial sludge, respectively. While air stripping and adsorption remove organic chemicals from wastewater and help meet effluent limitations, they merely transfer the pollutants to other media (i.e., directly to the atmosphere and to the land or atmosphere indirectly via sludge). In solving one problem, care must be taken to avoid exacerbating or creating other problems, which may be as bad as the one solved.

The U.S. Environmental Protection Agency (EPA) recently conducted a study (U.S. EPA, 1985) to assess the magnitude and nature of the ambient air toxics problem in the United States. Two conclusions from this study bear on the cross-media transfer of pollutants, especially from municipal wastewater treatment facilities. The first was that nontraditional sources of air toxics, such as publicly owned treatment works (POTWs)—what used to be called municipal wastewater treatment plants—and hazardous waste treatment, storage, and disposal facilities (TSDFs), may pose important risks in some locations. Findings from the study suggested that some POTWs with industrial contributions may emit large amounts of volatile compounds. The second was that as a broad category of activities, combustion/incineration may be the largest single source of air toxics risk. As a waste management tool, incineration is used for disposal of sludges, municipal solid wastes, and hazardous wastes.

The second illustration focuses on sludge production and disposal. Each process in a wastewater treatment system produces solids—or sludge—that require additional handling, stabilization, and disposal. The quantities of sludge that are produced at a POTW are a function of the characteristics of the influent wastewater, the operation of the treatment process, and the type and quantity of any chemicals that are used. Reasonable values of sludge production can be estimated and are presented in Table 2.1.

Table 2.1
Estimated Sludge Production From Wastewater Treatment

Process	Production (1)	
	lbs/mil gal (2)	gals/mil gal (3)
Primary Treatment	600 - 1,300	2,400 - 4,000
Secondary Treatment - Activated Sludge	600 - 900	15,000 - 20,000

Tertiary Treatment (4)
- Phosphorus Removal
  - with lime
  - with alum
- Ammonia Oxidation
  (Nitrification)
	
	2,500 - 6,800
	1,500 - 2,000
	
	90
		
		50,000 - 63,000
		10,000 - 14,000
		
		2,000

(1) Reasonable values resulting from the treatment of municipal wastewater; values obtained from many sources.

(2) Pounds of dry solids resulting from the treatment of one million gallons of wastewater.

(3) Gallons of sludge resulting from the treatment of one million gallons of wastewater.

(4) Treatment of secondary effluent to achieve specific effluent standards or water quality goals.

The values in Table 2.1 indicate that the quantities of sludge produced by the primary, secondary, and tertiary treatment processes generally increase as the degree of treatment increases. This is particularly obvious when the data concerning the gallons of sludge produced are scanned. Currently between 6.5 and 7 million dry metric tons of wastewater sludge are generated annually in the United States. As a result of increased water pollution control efforts, this quantity may increase to between 10 and 14 million dry metric tons annually.

The comparative energy requirements associated with the wastewater treatment processes also are interesting; see Table 2.2 for data adapted from Owen (1982). Secondary and tertiary processes are the most energy-intensive processes with the activated sludge process being the secondary treatment process that requires large amounts of energy for mixing and aeration.

The overall costs of sludge management are relevant to this discus-

Table 2.2
Relative Energy Consumption of Wastewater Treatment Processes

Process	Estimated Energy Consumption* (billion BTU/yr)
Primary Treatment	1.5
Secondary Treatment	
- Activated Sludge	68
Tertiary Treatment	
- Phosphorus Removal	42
- Nitrification	55
- Activated Carbon	90
Chlorination	30

*Unit process energy requirements for a 30 million gallon per day municipal treatment plant (POTW).

sion. In terms of volume of wastewater treated, the quantities of sludge produced are very small—in the range of 0.02 to 0.08 gallons of sludge produced per gallon of wastewater treated. Unfortunately the costs of sludge management are not in the same proportion. At an average treatment plant, the cost of sludge handling and management can be about 40 percent of planning and construction costs and near 50 percent of operation costs. In this example, the linear wastewater management approach increases the quantity of sludge to be managed, the energy required, and the cost of waste management considerably.

REGULATORY PERSPECTIVE

With minor exceptions, the Congress perpetuates linear waste management approaches and lack of cross-media concerns by passing legislation that results in regulations to control specific environmental problems. Examples are noted in Table 2.3. The legislation and resulting regulations emphasize the management of a specific medium (air, water, and oceans) or problem (hazardous wastes, pesticides, and abandoned sites). This emphasis is not inappropriate since it is a particular concern that has identified the need for better protection of public health and the environment. However, this single-effort or single-medium focus

Table 2.3
**Environmental Control Legislation Promoting Linear Waste Management
and Pollution Control**

Legislation	Primary Type of Control or Management
Clean Air Act	air pollution control
Federal Water Pollution Control Act and Amendments	water pollution control
Clean Water Act	water pollution control
Resource Conservation and Recovery Act	hazardous wastes
Marine Protection, Research and Sanctuaries Act	ocean disposal
Comprehensive Environmental Response, Compensation, and Liability Act	abandoned hazardous waste disposal sites
Safe Drinking Water Act	potable water

unduly limits consideration of cross-media concerns, such as the residues generated by water and air pollution control processes, volatiles and gases emitted from stripping towers and aeration basins, and bioaccumulation of organics and inorganics when wastes are disposed of in the terrestrial and ocean environments.

Groundwater contamination represents another cross-media problem that can occur as a result of a linear waste management mentality. Reports of groundwater contamination increase in both number and severity. Evaluations of these reports commonly reveal that the contamination is a result of lesser attention to the disposal of residues (sludges, industrial wastes, pesticides, and solvents) and inadequate understanding of the assimilative capacity of soils. Public agency responsibilities overlap or are inadequate; and until recently, no specific regulations controlled this problem. The 1984 Amendments to the Resource Recovery and Conservation Act (RCRA) have provided an important thrust to minimize groundwater contamination by attempting to control the source of possible contamination: waste piles and impoundments, landfills, and underground storage tanks.

The medium-by-medium regulatory approach also results in conflicts and inadequate cross-media concerns. Two examples illustrate this problem (National Advisory Committee on Oceans and Atmosphere, 1981): (1) incineration and disposal of wastes containing carcinogens and (2) the disposal of cadmium-containing wastes.

To paraphrase from these examples, RCRA encourages the incineration of hazardous wastes that contain carcinogens while the Clean Air Act discourages such incineration. In addition, the RCRA regulations do not address the problem of airborne carcinogens that may be released and eventually return to the land or water.

With respect to cadmium, there are rigorous criteria governing the land application of cadmium-containing wastes, such as sludges and industrial wastes. However, there are no air emission standards for cadmium even though the EPA estimates that 30 percent of the cadmium that enters an incinerator goes into the atmosphere and ultimately returns to the land or water. Thus, different regulations have resulted in unequal levels of protection for human health and the environment depending upon the disposal medium.

Owing to the single-medium focus of environmental legislation, environmental regulatory agencies face a formidable task in assessing multi-media concerns and in providing consistent levels of protection. This focus does not adequately acknowledge the interactions among the air, water, and terrestrial environments. Future regulations must reflect an understanding that we are dealing with an ecosystem, the multi-media implications can be significant, and the single-medium control and single-problem focus will continue to allow some serious environmental problems to "fall through the cracks."

CIRCULAR WASTE MANAGEMENT

Circular waste management includes approaches that consider recovery and reuse and the use of land as a waste management alternative. The latter consideration recognizes that most of the products humans use and which generate waste originate from the land (food, fuel, ores, fiber, and shelter); the soil has an assimilative capacity for wastes and residues; and the bulk of the constituents (water, nutrients, trace elements, and organics) are beneficial when applied to the soil when the soil assimilative capacity is not exceeded. Unfortunately, this waste-management approach had been deemphasized in the earlier part of this century.

Animal production offers an opportunity to examine the alteration of a natural cycle—the circular approach—and the resultant environmental effects (Loehr, 1984). The basic cycle consists of the land providing feed for the animals, whose waste is returned to the land to help produce more feed. However, in modern agriculture, substantial quantities of fertilizer, pesticides, and external energy are necessary to obtain desired crop and animal production levels. As long as the resultant animal manures are utilized in the cycle, the cycle remains essentially closed and environmental concerns related to waste management are minimal. However, when there is a break in the cycle or improper management of one of the components, environmental problems increase.

For instance, when the wastes are allowed to accumulate prior to application to the land, undesirable odors can result and runoff can cause surface water pollution. Improper management of the wastes when applied to the land also can result in groundwater pollution. The further from the basic cycle the situation is permitted to go, the more unbalanced the situation becomes; and the greater the waste management problems and costs to maintain desired environmental quality conditions. The better solution to animal waste management lies in keeping to the basic cycle as much as possible, and in the utilization of the residues rather than in wasting or losing them.

In the last 15 years, there has been a concerted effort to encourage greater use of the land as a waste management alternative and to encourage water conservation and water and waste reuse. This has resulted from the passage of Public Law 92–500—the amendments to the Federal Water Pollution Control Act—in 1972. A key goal of the legislation was "to restore and maintain the chemical, physical, and biological integrity of the Nation's waters." To achieve this goal, focus was placed on the development of technology necessary to eliminate "the discharge of pollutants into the navigable waters" of the United States. This became the "zero discharge" alternative—meaning the goal was no discharge of wastewaters to surface waters.

Land treatment of a waste is a technology that can achieve "zero discharge" of wastes through application of the wastes to the soil. Land treatment was to be considered in all cases because of the effectiveness and the lesser costs associated with this technology. Other quickly realized attributes of this technology were: (1) there is no residual sludge that requires management—any increases in biomass or inorganic precipitates that occur remain in the soil; (2) phosphorus and nitrogen removals occur automatically in the soil by natural chemical and biological reactions, thus avoiding the need for tertiary treatment processes; and (3) the greater retention time of applied wastes in the soil allows greater removals of potentially toxic and recalcitrant organics than occur in conventional waste treatment systems.

The use of land treatment technologies for wastewaters, sludges, and industrial wastes grew slowly in part due to the small number of environmental engineers and regulatory personnel who were familiar with or understood the land treatment options and in part by the initial lack of sound technical material and guidance documents. The use accelerated as a result of educational and training programs that were developed (Loehr et al., 1979) and the large numbers of technical guidance documents that have become available. Examples include Overcash and Paul (1979), U.S. EPA (1981), Page et al. (1983), and Fuller and Warrick (1985).

Considerable impetus was given to the use of land treatment in a memo by EPA's then-administrator Douglas Costle (1977). The memo noted:

At the time PL 92–500 was enacted, it was the intent of Congress to encourage to the extent possible the development of wastewater management policies that are consistent with the fundamental ecological principle that all materials should be returned to the cycles from which they were generated. Particular attention should be given to wastewater treatment processes that renovate and reuse wastewater and recycle the organic matter and nutrients in a beneficial manner. Therefore the Agency will press vigorously for publicly owned treatment works to utilize land treatment processes to reclaim and recycle wastewater.

The memo also noted that (1) reliable wastewater treatment processes that utilize land treatment concepts to recycle resources through agriculture, silviculture, and aquaculture practices are available and (2) the utilization of land treatment has the potential for saving billions of dollars of construction grant dollars as compared to conventional municipal wastewater treatment facilities.

As a result of PL 92–500, the technical guidance material now available, the increased number of environmental engineers who have been educated in the appropriate use of land treatment technologies, and the considerable experience that has been obtained from full-scale systems, there has been a resurgence in circular waste management approaches and the use of the land as a waste management alternative.

The results of these land treatment systems have been positive. At properly designed and operated land treatment sites, groundwater contamination has not occurred, disease transmission has not occurred, nuisance conditions have been few, and plant uptake of constituents in the applied waste has not resulted in public health problems. Appropriate emphasis on proper design and proper operation is just as important in land treatment systems as it is in traditional wastewater treatment facilities. Inadequate design and operation produce undesirable and unintended results and substandard treatment performance in both sorts of systems.

LAND TREATMENT AND LAND DISPOSAL

Although there has been considerable success with land treatment technologies and properly designed land treatment systems can be protective of human health and the environment, these facts have not yet been totally understood and accepted. This is illustrated by statements in the 1984 Amendments to RCRA. In RCRA as amended, land disposal is defined as the placement of a hazardous waste in a "land-fill, surface impoundment, waste pile, injection well, land treatment facility, salt dome formation or underground mine or cave." This definition does not recognize the unique differences, which are considerable, between land treatment and the other disposal processes. Of the noted processes, only land treatment is a process that will "treat" the applied wastes and actually reduce the pollutional or hazardous nature of the wastes. The other processes are storage processes in which there is little, if any, transformation that in any way reduces the pollutional or hazardous constituents in the wastes.

Land treatment is a managed treatment and ultimate disposal process that involves the controlled application of a waste to a soil or soil-vegetation system. The wastes are applied to the surface or mixed with the upper zone—0–1 feet or 0–0.3 meters—of soil. The objective of land treatment is the biological degradation of organic waste constituents and the immobilization of inorganic waste constituents within the treatment zone. Municipal wastewaters and sludges, as well as industrial wastes, can be treated using this process (Loehr and Overcash, 1985).

Land treatment should not be confused with the indiscriminate dumping of waste on land or in ponds, landfills, deep well injection, or arid region waste impoundments. The design goals, long-term impact, and degree of treatment of these other terrestrial systems are very different from those of proper land treatment.

Land treatment relies on the dynamic physical, chemical, and biological processes occurring in the soil. As a result, the applied wastes are degraded, transformed, or immobilized. At a land treatment site, wastes are applied to soil at rates—or over such limited time spans—such that no land is irreversibly removed from a defined use. After use for waste application, the land should be able to be returned to conditions suitable for beneficial uses such as crop production.

Although land treatment is primarily a treatment process, it is also a disposal process since some of the applied constituents and certain waste by-products remain at the site at closure. Land treatment differs from land disposal processes such as landfills in that, with land treatment, the assimilative capacity of the soil is used to detoxify, immobilize, and degrade all or a portion of the applied waste. Landfills are containments that store hazardous wastes and control the migration of the waste or by-products from the landfill sites. Liners are not required with land treatment. Some of the major differences between land treatment and landfills are noted in Table 2.4.

Land treatment facilities are representative of circular waste man-

Table 2.4
Differences Between Land Treatment and Landfills

Item	Land Treatment	Landfill
Waste Treatment Occurs	Yes	No
General Concept	Treatment (degrada-tion, transformation, and immobilization)	Containment
Waste Quantity	Limited to the assim-ilative capacity of the soil by adjusting waste loading rate and frequency	Unlimited and not related to the assimilative capacity of the soil
Waste Application Method	Incorporation into the soil	Not mixed with soil
Liquids Acceptable	Yes	No
Monitoring	Soil cores, soil pore water, groundwater	Leak detection, groundwater
Liner Needed	No	Yes
Leachate Collection and Treatment	None	Needed
Run-on and Runoff Control	Yes	Yes
Waste Degradation	Considerable	Little
Waste Immobilization	Yes	Only due to liner
Post-Closure Care	Minimal	Long-term

agement systems. Land treatment recycles and reuses applied constit-uents, does not result in secondary by-products—such as sludge—that require additional management, and can result in lower overall waste management costs. On the other hand, landfills represent a linear waste management system. Additional components such as single and double liners, leachate collection and treatment systems, gas vents, and well-designed caps are added to landfills in an attempt to protect human health and the environment. Land disposal processes such as surface impoundments, waste piles, and landfills tend to abuse or over-load—rather than use—the soil assimilative capacity. In contrast, land treatment facilities are designed and operated to use and not exceed the soil assimilative capacity.

LAND-BASED ENVIRONMENTAL QUALITY LIMITS

The increased use of land as a waste management alternative requires an evaluation of appropriate environmental quality limits to assure that this option is protective of human health and the environment. Such limits also help establish the level and type of treatment that is needed. The "how clean is clean?" question is part of this evaluation. The subsequent discussion is not intended to address this question in detail; rather, it is intended to identify options that may be appropriate for situations where land treatment or contaminated soil cleanup is being considered.

Decisions concerning environmental quality limits are decisions re-lating to risk. Since all risks cannot be reduced to zero, the identification of suitable environmental quality limits is the identification of risks that are judged to be socially acceptable. It is important to identify whether the risks are borne voluntarily or involuntarily. Risks that an individual must bear involuntarily are risks that the government has the greatest responsibility to regulate. Most of the risks that occur when land is used as a waste management alternative are those that are borne involuntarily by the public.

In assessing risk it is necessary to define the conditions of exposure, identify the adverse effects, relate exposure with effect, and estimate overall risk (Lowrance, 1976). Although this represents the reasonable way of establishing environmental quality limits, less ideal approaches are more commonly used.

Simplistically, management of risks and development of environ-mental quality limits have followed one of three separate procedures: ban the activity, process, or material; reduce the activity or exposure to the pollutant as much as possible; and conduct a thorough risk-benefit analysis to allow a fuller appreciation of all the factors in-volved. Reducing the exposure is the more common procedure used to determine acceptable limits. This is accomplished by establishing technology-based standards or environment-based criteria.

For land-based waste management alternatives, both approaches have been used. For example, because landfills overload the waste assimi-lative capacity of a site, technology-based controls are the primary en-vironmental control measures. These are liners to minimize leakage from the landfill, leachate collection and treatment systems to properly manage leachate that does occur, and caps and run-on diversions to minimize precipitation input into the landfill.

In comparison, land treatment systems use but do not overload the waste assimilative capacity of a site. The technological controls utilize the degradation and immobilization processes that occur in the soil. In this manner, environment-based criteria result in a waste application rate that does not exceed the soil assimilative capacity.

The technological bases for both landfill and land treatment controls are reasonably well understood. While these controls can be quite effective, they do not prevent some percolation of liquid from these sites. An unresolved concern is what environmental criteria should be applied to determine whether the constituents in the percolate will have an unacceptably adverse effect on human health and the environment.

The principle of de minimis can be considered (Weinberg, 1986; Whipple, 1986). The principle is that "one should not worry about any additional manmade exposure as long as the manmade exposure is small compared to the natural exposure" (Weinberg, 1986). It is argued that an additional exposure that is small compared to the natural background ought to be acceptable.

The term de minimis is used in law to describe trivial issues not deserving of a court's time and attention. When applied to health and safety, the term refers to a risk that avoids regulatory attention by virtue of its small size. A de minimis rationale can be used to determine a regulatory standard or to decide that no standard is required. A de minimis approach can provide a means for simplifying the regulatory process, especially for low-risk constituents that are determined to be low priority from the regulatory standpoint. The approach also can provide a policy solution to concerns that are not easily decided on the basis of scientific information.

The application of the de minimis approach to land-based waste management process performance has not been attempted as yet. To do so would require a significant sampling and analysis effort to determine the soil and groundwater concentration of the diverse constituents that may be in a land-applied waste. A careful screening effort to discern which chemicals are likely to be of concern at a land-based site would reduce the sampling and analysis effort to more manageable levels. These chemicals are those that are highly mobile, are toxic in low concentrations, and may bioaccumulate.

It will also be necessary to determine a satisfactory de minimis concentration. For radiation (Weinberg, 1986), one might choose such a level as the standard deviation of the natural background, which turns out to be about 20 percent of the mean background. For some constituent concentrations in percolate, leachate, soil, or groundwater, the permissible levels might be set at average local, regional, or national background concentrations. This would avoid allowing higher concentrations for which greater uncertainty about the human health and environment effect might exist. For constituents of greater concern such as carcinogens, permissible levels might be set at some fraction of background, perhaps at 20 to 50 percent.

The issue of what environmental criteria should be used to assure adequate control at land-based waste management sites requires significant discussion and evaluation. Experience indicates that past technological controls at land-based waste storage facilities—such as landfills, waste piles, lagoons, and impoundments—are not always protective of human health. To design better controls, designation of protective environmental criteria are needed.

SUMMARY

Sound management of potential threats to human health and the environment is difficult because of regulatory inconsistencies, frequent benign neglect of multi-media transfers of pollutants, and poor definition of environmental criteria for land-based waste management alternatives.

EPA is the federal agency responsible for pollution control and has different legislative mandates and constraints for such control. For instance, EPA is charged with the implementation of eight major environmental statutes, each dealing with a different aspect of environmental protection. Some of these statutes require or allow regulatory decisions based on risk reduction. Others require control of toxic pollutants based on available technology and cost instead of risk reduction.

Program integration continues to be a problem at EPA because of these diverse mandates. As a result, there can be unwitting transfer of pollutants from one medium to another as a result of an adopted pollution control technology, a narrow medium or problem focus, and a minimum concern with critical multi-media environmental concerns.

The use of land as a waste management alternative will continue to increase. Such use can help provide an environmentally sound solution for the treatment and disposal of many wastes. Unfortunately, to date it is noted that the assimilative capacity of the soil continues to be poorly understood and reliance commonly has been placed on containment technologies that have been developed with only vague knowledge of suitable environmental criteria that are to be achieved.

To overcome these difficulties, it is important that:

1. The single-problem or single-medium approach to waste management be deemphasized. A more coherent multi-media approach that recognizes cross-media transfer of pollutants is badly needed.

2. The legislative and regulatory frameworks require an evaluation of all waste management options when an environmental problem requires solution. The framework should seek a balanced and equitable allocation of costs for multi-media impacts. There should be coordinated management of gaseous, liquid, and solid materials so that problems are not simply shifted from one medium to another.

3. Circular rather than linear waste management approaches must receive greater emphasis. Reuse, recovery, reducing waste generation, and the use of the soil assimilative capacity are more technically effective and likely more cost-effective waste management approaches than the traditional approaches that add treatment processes and create sludges and other residues that require further management.

4. The assimilative capacity of the soil should be more adequately defined so as to learn how to use—but not abuse—this medium for waste management.

5. Definitive environmental criteria and quality limits should be developed for soil and groundwater when the land is used as a waste management alternative.

BIBLIOGRAPHY

Cairns, John, Jr. 1986. "Management of Water Quality and Natural Habitats to Enhance Both Human and Wildlife Needs." In *Managing Water Resources*, John Cairns, Jr. and Ruth Patrick, eds., New York: Praeger Publishers.

Costle, Douglas. 1977. "EPA Policy on Land Treatment of Municipal Wastewaters." Memorandum issued to Assistant Administrators and Regional Administrators, U.S. Environmental Protection Agency, Washington, D.C., October 3.

Fuhrman, R. E. 1984. "History of Water Pollution Control." *Journal Water Pollution Control Federation*, 56: 306–313.

Fuller, W. H. and A. W. Warrick. 1985. *Soils in Waste Treatment and Utilization*, Vols. I and II. Boca Raton, Fla.: CRC Press.

Loehr, R. C. 1984. *Pollution Control for Agriculture*, 2nd Ed. New York: Academic Press.

Loehr, R. C., W. J. Jewell, J. D. Novak, W. W. Clarkson, and G. S. Friedman. 1979. *Land Application of Wastes*, Vols. I and II. New York: Van Nostrand Reinhold.

Loehr, R. C. and M. R. Overcash. 1985. "Land Treatment of Wastes: Concepts and General Design," *Journal of Environmental Engineering Division* (American Society of Civil Engineers) 111: 141–160.

Lowrance, W. W. 1976. *Of Acceptable Risk*. Los Altos: Wilham Kaufmann.

National Advisory Committee on Oceans and Atmosphere. 1981. "The Role of the Ocean in a Waste Management Strategy." A special report to the President and the Congress, Superintendent of Documents. Washington, D.C.: U.S. Government Printing Office.

Overcash, M. R. and D. Paul. 1979. *Design of Land Treatment for Industrial Wastes.* Ann Arbor, Mich.: Ann Arbor Science Publishers.

Owen, W. F. 1982. *Energy in Wastewater Treatment.* Englewood Cliffs, N.J.: Prentice-Hall.

Page, A. L., T. L. Gleason, J. E. Smith, J. K. Iskander, and L. E. Sommers. 1983. *Utilization of Municipal Wastewater and Sludge on Land.* Riverside: University of California.

U.S. Environmental Protection Agency. 1981. "Process Design Manual—Land Treatment of Municipal Waste-water." EPA publication no. 625/1–81–013, Center for Environmental Research Information, Cincinnati, Ohio.

_____. 1985. "The Air Toxics Problem in the United States: An Analysis of Cancer Risks for Selected Pollutants." Office of Air and Radiation and Office of Policy, Planning and Evaluation, publication no. EPA–450/1–85–001, Washington, D.C., May.

Weinberg, A. M. 1986. "Science and Its Limits: The Regulator's Dilemma." In *Hazards: Technology and Fairness,* National Academy of Engineering, Series on Technology and Social Priorities. Washington, D.C.: National Academy Press.

Whipple, C. 1986. "Dealing With Uncertainty About Risk in Risk Management." In *Hazards: Technology and Fairness,* National Academy of Engineering, Series on Technology and Social Priorities. Washington, D.C.: National Academy Press.

3

Effective Toxics Management:
A Multi-Media Perspective
David L. Morell

ABSTRACT

For over 15 years, the United States has pursued abatement of conventional environmental pollutants, with some success, through monomedium statutes and regulations. These laws have been weakest in their attention to cross-media effects and land use. As a result, the toxics crisis finds us unable to cope effectively with multi-media human health risks. Resultant public outcry for action encounters inadequate laws and inept institutions. Public frustration grows; government and industry credibility dwindle.

Specific examples are presented of the environmental effects of these monomedium statutes. A broader perspective sees the interweaving of three fundamental components of an environmental strategy: hazardous waste management, groundwater quality, and surface water supplies. Finally, a new approach is offered to blend the traditional approaches of environmental regulation into local decisions on risk management, using national standards and cross-media risk assessment procedures to define local needs for cleanup, preservation, and land development.

Key Words: toxics, hazardous waste treatment and disposal, Superfund, groundwater contamination, air toxics, cleanup, risk assessment, risk management, Integrated Environmental Management Project

INTRODUCTION

The entire Dubos Center Land Use Management Forum is an exciting and creative attempt to explore uncharted territory: land-use decision making from a cross-media perspective. The issues are intense and complex. As a result, unraveling this disjointed web of environmental interactions into some kind of comprehensible pattern of events and causes becomes extraordinarily difficult. In the best ecological tradition of Dr. René Dubos, everything is connected to everything else. This chapter is admittedly a crude, first approximation of what eventually will be required.

Our nation's principal environmental statutes all emerged through political response to specific perceived problems of environmental degradation. Localities, states, and eventually the U.S. Congress acted in response to political pressures to act. These pressures, almost without exception, focused on a single medium: air pollution in Los Angeles or New Jersey; a river on fire in Ohio; a lake in Oregon under stress from runoff.

In the spirit of the "issue-attention cycle," laws were passed and regulations were written to deal with these single-medium problems. Ambient air quality standards were set and, to some degree, enforced. New-source performance standards were set for new smokestacks' air emissions, and ditto for new automobiles. Similarly, National Pollutant Discharge Elimination System (NPDES) permits were issued to thousands of dischargers to the nation's navigable waters, and billions upon billions of federal dollars were spent to assist states and localities in construction of municipal wastewater treatment and collection systems. The 1970 Clean Air Act and the 1977 Clean Water Act—earlier termed the 1972 Amendments to the Federal Water Pollution Control Act—were the dominant national regulatory instruments, supplemented of course by the Toxic Substances Control Act, Pesticides Act, related acts, and other (rather minor) approaches which reached beyond the single-medium perspective adopted by the environmental pressure groups, by the Congress, and therefore by the Environmental Protection Agency.

In 1974, interestingly, EPA decided to bifurcate its previous Office of Air and Water Programs, then under the control of a single assistant administrator. Never since then has the EPA's own structure approached even this semblance of cross-media management.

These 1970s environmental regulatory programs have accomplished much, of course. The air is indeed cleaner; so too is the water. However, much of this success was achieved through cross-media transfers of pollutants—to the land and the groundwater in particular, but also between the air and water media. Control technologies required under the air and water acts rarely if ever actually "destroyed" the pollutants; they simply changed their form, or shifted their location, or altered their time horizon.

A scrubber or flue gas desulfurization (FGD) system at a coal-burning power plant, for example, can indeed remove a great deal of the sulfur pollutants from the stack gas. They enter a wet limestone sludge, which then gets placed on the land. The same goes for the ash from an incinerator. A wastewater treatment system at a large industrial facility indeed produces water effluents suitable for discharge to the receiving surface water body. It does so, however, by concentrating the metals into a sludge, headed for land disposal and—much too often—for later leaching into nearby groundwater. Even a traditional municipal sewage treatment plant produces enormous volumes of sludge requiring "disposal" of some kind: on or in the land or sometimes into the air through incineration. In essence, the game plan frequently seems to be: "We keep moving the pollutants around."

Success in dealing with the conventional air and water pollutants was achieved at a very high cost. At the very close of the 1970s, we began to perceive our hazardous waste crisis. From Love Canal to the Valley of the Drums, and from Times Beach or the Chemical Control Corporation to the Stringfellow Acid Pits, our legacy of industrial mismanagement of toxic wastes suddenly thrust itself into the national consciousness. These industrial wastes—acids, heavy metals, organic solvents, still bottoms, and contaminated sludges and soils—were the dark backside of our productive economy.

In the early 1980s, Americans came to see that these toxics were everywhere: in all the media. Toxics were clearly on the land. The EPA initially estimated 15,000 to 30,000 dump sites would require remedial action; the mid–1988 figure was 29,707 such sites (U.S. EPA, 1988). The Congressional Office of Technology Assessment (OTA) estimated public-sector cost for cleanup of $100 billion (U.S. OTA 1986), plus untold additional direct corporate dollars. Toxics were in the air; and toxics were clearly in groundwater. We came to understand that the traditional grand old principle of sanitary engineering—that filtration of pollutants through the soils will protect groundwater from contamination—did not apply to organic chemicals. Toxics were in our waters, particularly from weakly regulated industrial discharges into municipal sewerage systems.

Again, the political system fumbled toward a response; and again, despite the updated terminology that avoided direct reference to the several media, response was single-medium-focused. The 1976 Resource Conservation and Recovery Act, until then an underused statute on municipal solid wastes (or garbage), was turned into EPA's major tool for its attempts at hazardous waste management. Its focus was almost exclusively on land disposal. Congressional revisions to RCRA in November 1984 strengthened it greatly.

Interestingly, the thrust now is to transition rapidly away from land disposal of hazardous wastes and instead, toward their treatment, primarily through industrial wastewater techniques. In other words, we have come full circle from the 1972 Water Act's formal goal of "zero discharge of pollutants to the nation's navigable waters" by 1985 to, in essence, "phase out land disposal of hazardous wastes by treating liquid waste streams to concentrate the pollutants into sludges and then discharging the treated effluent to surface waters."

In sum, our approach to modern environmental management in the United States for nearly two decades has evidenced two major conceptual gaps: a needed cross-media focus and a comprehension of the impact of land use on environmental actions and environmental results. Cross-media problems have already been noted. The lack of focus on land use was justified, federally, by the shibboleth that the states—more or less—were in charge: "Land use is the domain of the states, and especially of local governments." As a result, one federal statute after another focused excessively on technological imperatives. In essence, EPA approached being a "PAA" (Pollution Abatement Agency) rather than a true environmental protection agency, with a strong comprehension of the overall environmental impacts of land development on the ambient environment in all of its important multi-media dimensions.

The Dubos Center Land Use Management Forum has a unique opportunity to redress this imbalance, and to seek to integrate the traditional approaches to environmental management with both of these heretofore regrettably absent perspectives: land use and cross-media.

MONOMEDIUM STATUTES, LAND-USE IMPLICATIONS, AND ENVIRONMENTAL EFFECTS

How serious are the cross-media effects of particular land development decisions? And how do the monomedium statutes and regulations that govern our regulatory and permitting process—and therefore determine, in large measure, what gets built where—affect development decisions? Let us look first at a few sporadic, specific examples of this phenomenon, and then shift toward a somewhat broader perspective.

NO_x Controls and Hazardous Waste Incineration

Clearly, land disposal of hazardous waste solvents—TCE, PCE, TCA, and the whole alphanumeric lexicon—has to be brought to a halt. Impacts from landfills and surface impoundments and deep wells are too great on groundwater and on air. Many of these solvent wastes can be recycled; many millions of gallons in the near term, however, need to be destroyed instead through thermal treatment, or incineration.

In an area such as Los Angeles, which currently generates several hundred thousand tons of incineratable hazardous wastes annually, incineration would represent a distinct environmental improvement to existing patterns of land disposal and illegal disposal. Indeed, incineration of these wastes would reduce total air pollution—smog precursors, as well as toxic air pollutants—because these volatile organics now evaporate into the air at a high rate.

From the perspective of air toxics regulations, an incinerator could be sited within the Los Angeles air basin—leaving aside, for the moment, the ever-present issue of public resistance to any new facilities. This is simply to say that neither EPA, nor the California Air Resources Board, nor the South Coast Air Quality Management District has set applicable air emissions standards for most toxic air contaminants. The state agency has recently done so for benzene. So, few strict permit rules apply to a proposed hazardous waste incinerator, which is needed to improve Los Angeles's situation with respect to waste management of volatile organics.

Unfortunately, a conventional pollutant under the Clean Air Act—oxides of nitrogen, NO_x—stands squarely in the way of progress toward siting a hazardous waste incinerator in this area. The Los Angeles area is failing to attain the Clean Air Act's standards for NO_x—the major area in the United States to be classified "non-attainment" for this pollutant. If a facility has sufficient NO_x emissions as to exceed the threshold for New Source Review under the Clean Air Act, it cannot be built in Los Angeles without achieving an offset from other combustion sources. Many hazardous waste incinerators are likely to need such an offset.

Where are the available offsets? Given the overall stress on air quality in the Los Angeles basin, only the large refineries still hold sufficient NO_x offsets, acquired in their own improvements to their air emissions. Here the cross-media issues broaden further, for the refineries are unwilling to make their offsets available to anyone else, even for a socially—and environmentally—valuable project such as a new hazardous waste incinerator. There is, in the economists' jargon, essentially no market for offsets. Why are the oil companies so obstreperous? For very good and sound corporate reasons.

Large amounts of new oil have been discovered or projected in recent years off the coast of California, particularly in the Santa Maria Channel north of Santa Barbara. This oil's characteristics include a very high sulfur content—it is what is called "sour crude." Los Angeles's existing refineries are not equipped to process large volumes of such oil. They will need to undergo major retrofits to do so, and such retrofits will alter air emissions characteristics, particularly for NO_x. Therefore, the refineries will eventually need to use their own available offsets, and are unwilling to let them be diverted to anyone else for any other socially beneficial purpose.

So the siting of a hazardous waste incinerator that would reduce air pollution on a net basis in Los Angeles, and contribute markedly to resolving a serious hazardous waste problem, is stalled by the dictates of a conventional pollutant under the Clean Air Act, and entrapped in the multi-dimensional dynamics of offshore oil development.

Toxic Air Emissions from Sewage Treatment Plants

Sewage treatment plants are designed to treat sewage from domestic sources plus compatible wastes from industrial dischargers. For these specific purposes, they can and frequently do work extremely well.

Unfortunately, thousands of industrial dischargers across the country use available sewers for discharge of acids, bases, metals, and volatile organic wastes. These discharges are supposed to be controlled by the pretreatment programs of the individual sewage treatment plants. Finally—in 1984, after more than a decade of delay—EPA established national categorical pretreatment standards which cover only a narrow range of dischargers, mostly metal finishers and electroplaters.

In large measure, the inorganic pollutants are concentrated in the sludge from the sewage plants. This poses its own set of cross-media problems, since the sludges are then not usable for land fertilization and require special handling as a land disposal waste.

The toxic organic wastes in the sewer systems, however, often do not end up in the sludge. They are volatile, and thus evaporate into the air within the sewers or at the treatment plant or in the receiving water body after passing through the sewage treatment plant.

In its Integrated Environmental Management Project (IEMP) in the Philadelphia metropolitan area, EPA found the Northeast Philadelphia Sewage Treatment Plant to be the largest single source of air toxics in the entire area—more than any one of the oil refineries or chemical plants or auto plants nearby (U.S. EPA, 1986). Industries throughout the city in the preceding decade—responding to pressures for air emissions control at their own facilities—had shifted to greater sewering of these organic wastes.

Nowhere in the regulatory process had anyone asked: "What happens to these volatile organic chemicals once they enter the sewer?" The sewage treatment plant's NPDES permit does not cover air emissions, because it is issued under Section 402 of the Clean Water Act. Philadelphia Air Management Services had never considered a wastewater treatment plant to be a target of its regulations—presumably, they deal with water, not air. The same logic seems to have applied to EPA Region

III's Air Division. So the organics continued to be emitted from the sewage treatment plant.

In EPA's later Integrated Environmental Management Project in California's Santa Clara Valley or "Silicon Valley," researchers looked at the largest of the four sewage treatment plants there: the San Jose/Santa Clara Water Pollution Control Plant. This facility discharges more than 100 million gallons per day of treated effluent to the southern portion of San Francisco Bay and receives regular discharges from some 400 tributary industrial users—each of which is covered under some kind of local pretreatment permit.

Air emissions analysis showed that this plant was not a particularly large source, owing to the nature of its industrial influent. It was, however, of a sufficient scale to be added to the 21 largest air emissions sources, including semiconductor factories, as the universe of air toxics analysis for the IEMP being conducted by the Bay Area Air Quality Management District.

In recognition of the air emissions issue, the Palo Alto/Mountain View Water Pollution Control Plant in the same area—with some 80 industrial users under pretreatment permit—began in 1985 to require each discharger to prepare a comprehensive Solvents Management Plan, setting forth details on its solvents use, storage, disposal, and sewer discharge of these organic pollutants.

Superfund: Hauling the Remedial Wastes Around

Another aspect of the complex land use/cross-media problem emerges from the national remedial action program under Superfund. To date, most of the cleanups have simply involved digging up one old dump site and hauling it to another—hopefully, one that is not yet leaking. Wastes from Chemical Control Corporation in Elizabeth, New Jersey, were taken to the CECOS landfill in Niagara Falls, New York. It later began to leak. Wastes from John Stringfellow's Acid Pits near Glen Avon, California, were hauled to the BKK Landfill in Los Angeles County. In November 1984, BKK was closed due to both leachate and toxic air emissions.

What are the cross-media impacts of this program? Leaks in one place stop, as the old wastes are removed. But air emissions occur en route to the new dump site, along with transportation risks. At the new facility, the same set of problems can eventually resume that presumably were to be avoided through the initial remedial action.

At some future point, one presumes, a whole new cross-media paradigm will have to be introduced into these Superfund remedial action decisions. While the hazard ranking system (HRS) model now used to set priorities for the national priority list (NPL) includes effects from several media (U.S. EPA, 1984b), its overwhelming focus remains on groundwater effects.

Instead, risk management can begin to take hold. This would require, for example, asking about the actual routes of exposure associated with a particular Superfund site, about probable concentrations of contaminants in each exposure pathway, and about the apparent toxicological potency of these various contaminants. Such an approach lies at the heart of EPA's IEMP work, but is a far cry from current procedures under the HRS, where no account is taken of either probable concentrations or potency. Each chemical is assumed to be full strength and equally dangerous.

As a result, the Superfund process has concentrated on attempts—so often, to date, with minimal success—to control groundwater leachate from dump sites. Yet in many cases, no one is being hurt by contamination through this route since nearby residents are drinking not from groundwater sources but from surface water supplies—typically chlorinated and containing trihalomethane (THM) by-products, another cross-media issue. The dump's impact on groundwater resources is real, but not perhaps particularly harmful to public health. Yet regulatory posture and public outcry are mesmerized by its leachate.

In contrast, little attention has been paid under either Superfund or RCRA to the air emissions from these facilities. Here, indeed, real harm may be occurring, particularly through night air drainage of airborne contaminants during periods when almost everyone is at home. For example, vinyl chloride air emissions from a dump site may be far more dangerous than any of its groundwater leaks. Gas collection systems and population relocation might be preferable alternatives to French drains and slurry walls, were actual public health protection the true goal of a cross-media environmental protection policy, rather than actions taken in response to immediate public perceptions of danger.

Moreover, under a risk management framework more attention would be paid to private wells serving individual households in the vicinity of hazardous waste dump sites. These wells exist by the thousands across the country, and have been found contaminated from Long Island and New Jersey to Oregon and California. Discovery of 35 contaminated private wells in Mountain View, California, in 1984—with resultant public outcry and political pressure in an election year—led to EPA's decision to propose to add 19 Superfund sites in Santa Clara County to the NPL—more than in any other county in the United States. There is no evidence that the public water supplies in Mountain View or nearby areas have significant contamination. In fact, they draw from a deeper aquifer, protected from above to date by a large clay barrier.

Private wells are doubly vulnerable from a risk management perspective. These wells are typically shallow, not deep, while the plumes of groundwater contamination are shallow in most cases, particularly at higher contaminant concentrations. Moreover, private wells are not regularly monitored for contamination, in contrast to many public water supply wells. Such monitoring, of course, provides tremendous periodic protection from risk associated with ingestion of contaminated water.

This is not an argument against groundwater leachate controls around hazardous waste sites. Hardly. It is, however, an argument that our obviously scarce resources—regulatory capacity as well as economic—need to be arrayed where they will do the most good in terms of real public health protection. That requires an honest, hard look at risks—pollutants, exposure pathways, concentrations, sources, treatment, and monitoring options—at the big picture rather than just at traditional sanitary engineering waste treatment technologies and end-of-pipe facilities design.

Superfund: Discharging Treated Effluent from Cleanup

Once the soils from one hazardous waste cleanup activity have been removed to another dump—or incinerated or stabilized on-site—many remedial actions turn to cleanup of contaminated groundwater. Here another set of pollutant transfers becomes evident, raising further complications. Where are these pollutants, now in the groundwater, supposed to go? Which medium of the environment will willingly accept them?

One approach, seen increasingly, involves aeration of the contaminated groundwater, either through air stripping towers—evaporation assisted by technology of air flow—or through simple pumping into nearby channels and storm sewers. The volatile organics disperse from the water into the air.

Air pollution impacts from such cross-media transfers obviously depend on the initial concentrations in the contaminated groundwater. In the Santa Clara Valley, where most of the groundwater problem exists at ten or so parts per billion, dispersal into the air renders the contamination unfindable even by today's sophisticated monitoring and modeling techniques. An EPA study for the IEMP found no measurable impacts even at the single house closest to the largest extraction well. Most of the aeration in this area involves simple pumping and discharge to storm sewers, thence to creeks, and eventually to San Francisco Bay. Monitoring results show that all of the pollutants have volatilized before the effluent reaches the Bay. Higher plume concentrations at certain industrial sites where solvent tanks leaked into the groundwater—at Fairchild Camera and Instrument Co. in south San Jose, for example—have been treated with carbon filtration after pumping.

Siting of aeration towers to treat contaminated groundwater illustrates another aspect of the cross-media/land use/toxics dilemma. While the public clearly does not want toxics in their groundwater, nor in their drinking water, resistance to siting of stripping towers in locales such as the San Fernando Valley of Los Angeles has made remedial action very difficult. For several years, the Los Angeles Department of Water and Power's (DWP) attempts to remove TCE contamination from its groundwater supplies by siting new aeration towers were blunted by public resistance.

DWP's River Supply Conduit blending system combines groundwater containing TCE contamination with imported surface waters from the Owens Valley/Mono Lake Aqueduct—another multi-media environmental example, to be sure—to achieve an annual average TCE level of just under five parts per billion, the California "action level" for this chemical in the drinking water. The towers, once built, will lessen such levels of contamination.

At the Stringfellow Pits in Riverside County, California, the EPA remedial action program since 1984 has required pumping from the groundwater some 60,000 gallons per day of lightly contaminated liquids containing both organics and metal constituents. The acid pits in these were removed earlier to the BKK Landfill in Los Angeles County. For many months, this large volume of water was removed by truck, first to BKK and—after that hazardous waste landfill closed—to the Casmalia Resources hazardous waste landfill in Santa Barbara County, more than 200 miles away.

Beginning in 1985, EPA began construction of a new treatment plant at the Stringfellow site, to further reduce the concentrations of these pollutants. The intent was to sewer the effluent from this treatment system, having only the sludge left requiring land disposal.

Stringfellow wastes had become highly political, however. This was the very facility that had helped bring about the demise of Rita Lavelle and Anne Gorsuch Burford from EPA. So EPA's proposals to send the treated effluent into the nearby Orange County Sanitation District's sewer system met sharp resistance. "Would we have to close the beaches?" asked elected county supervisors.

In response, EPA presented information on the quality of the discharge involved: lightly contaminated groundwater under the Stringfellow site, treated at Stringfellow through tertiary techniques, then sewered into a 200 million gallons per day system with large industrial flows for further treatment in the Orange County sewage treatment plants prior to discharge to the Pacific Ocean. This discharge from the Stringfellow treatment system was shown to meet, indeed exceed, all applicable industrial pretreatment limits anywhere in this large sewerage system. By comparison with any significant discharger using the system, the new Stringfellow effluent would be cleaner by far. Eventually the Orange County resistance ended, providing one more example of the oddities of cross-media pollution controversy.

One further note of speculation on this case is directly relevant to land use. Some knowledgeable observers believe that the Orange County elected officials opposed this sewering concept for reasons having nothing to do directly with the quality of the treated Stringfellow effluent. Instead, they feared that, if the new treatment plant were sited at Stringfellow, in Riverside County, pressures would grow to extend an industrial sewer line—the Santa Ana Water Pollution Interceptor—from Orange County to that location. The area near Stringfellow remains mostly agricultural though very close to the overall Los Angeles-Orange County industrial complex. It is, in a word, highly developable land. If Orange County could keep the large interceptor away from that area, perhaps further land development would accrue to Orange County rather than to Riverside County.

Sewerage systems enter the remedial action-groundwater business in an additional context: response to leaking underground storage tanks. Modern approaches to this problem, as in Santa Clara County, require new double-walled protection around all new underground tanks, plus groundwater monitoring around all existing tanks. Tanks found leaking must then be replaced with the upgraded new version. As the groundwater monitoring wells are put in place, however, where is the water to be discharged? Volumes are small, but the water may, of course, be contaminated. The San Jose-Santa Clara Water Pollution Control Plant has refused to receive such pumped water. As a result, the groundwater has at times had to be discharged to trucks at high expense, or sent into storm sewers.

Similarly, once evidence of a leak has been discovered, the California Regional Water Quality Control Board—responsible for groundwater quality—requires the polluter to determine the extent of the plume of contamination, preparatory to devising a cleanup strategy. Monitoring wells are placed carefully in the area, outward from the initial finding of contamination, until all wells show no traces of contamination downgradient from the tank or spill. At the IBM site in San Jose, for example, where a large leak of TCA and Freon-113 took place in 1980, IBM has drilled in excess of 300 monitoring wells. Again, the water pollution plant has resisted accepting test pump water into its large sewerage system.

One final issue of cross-media impacts from groundwater cleanup takes one directly to the traditional resources questions on which environmental policy used to focus, prior to the toxics crisis of the 1980s. Extraction of groundwater to remove a few parts per billion of a chemical contaminant leads to pumping—and typically to waste—of enormous amounts of water. The program in Santa Clara County is termed "pump and purge," and became known colloquially in late 1985 in a U.S. House of Representatives Oversight and Investigations Subcommittee hearing in San Jose as "pump and dump."

At the IBM and Fairchild plumes of contamination alone, some 19 million gallons per day of groundwater are being extracted, pumped into storm sewers, and eventually make their way to San Francisco Bay. During this process, the few parts per billion of TCA, Freon, and other contaminants evaporate and disperse into the air. This amount of water is almost equal to the total being imported into the Santa Clara Valley through the South Bay Aqueduct and the Delta water system for recharge into the aquifer, in a several-decades-long successful attempt to quell subsidence. In the 1930–50 period, parts of San Jose sank 13 feet due to overdrafting.

Moreover, the quality of the groundwater being pumped and dumped—once the contaminants aerate—is far superior to the surface water being imported through the Delta, where water picks up high concentrations of natural organics and some pesticide residues. The resource implications of groundwater extraction for purposes of remedial action pose a further challenge to modern cross-media environmental protection and management policy.

Disposal of Contaminated Soil

As we explore whether single-walled gasoline, solvent, diesel, and wastewater tanks have leaked into the surrounding soil and groundwater, often the answer is "yes." In Santa Clara County, where the required monitoring programs are now widespread around several thousand existing underground tanks, some 50 percent or so of all tanks show signs of contamination nearby. What is then to be done with the contaminated soil?

One option, of course, is to haul it away to a certified hazardous waste landfill. First, this is very expensive. Second, it is fraught with the problems of all landfilling—both environmental impacts and resultant strict joint and several liability for the generator or owner of the soil.

Another option is aeration on site—depending, of course, on the level of contamination in the soil. Here permission from the local air quality management district is required; but it is difficult to obtain. Some dischargers apply for permission, and occasionally retest their soil to check on its status while the permit application is pending. Given the volatile nature of most of the soil contaminants typically found around gas tanks, the passage of time leads to lower and lower levels of residual contamination. This is aeration by delay in the regulatory process, perhaps. Then the soil can either be disposed in a regular sanitary landfill or retained on-site.

One additional—and probably unique—example from Santa Clara County illustrates the absurdities inherent in today's monomedium regulation of cross-media problems. Kaiser Cement Corporation operates a very large cement plant outside Cupertino, replete with an enormous rotary kiln fired 24 hours per day, 7 days per week at 1600°F or so. The kiln is fed with coal—thousands of tons per week—plus limestone from the local quarry and other constituents to make cement.

In its compliance with the local underground tank ordinance, Kaiser drilled monitoring wells as required near its own on-site diesel tanks. Evidence was found of leaks and soil contamination. The first and obvious response was to consider placing the diesel-contaminated soil into this hot kiln, where it would be totally destroyed with no impact whatsoever on nearby air quality. No one disputed the facts, but the air permit processing required for Kaiser to gain permission to do so was so onerous, time consuming, and expensive that the company decided instead simply to pay to have the dirt hauled away to a hazardous waste landfill. This hardly seems like a sensible 1980s solution to a problem of disposal of contaminated soil from a facility that actually has available the technical capacity to destroy it through incineration.

Integrated Industrial Waste Processing

Land development is certainly needed for one kind of new facility: hazardous waste treatment. These facilities are needed by society so that we can begin to treat the thousands of tons of hazardous wastes being produced annually, and thence be able finally to close the remaining landfills which pose such cross-media environmental risks. However, such facilities are precluded from development in many communities by siting controversy often incorporated in the "not in my backyard" or "NIMBY" syndrome.

Let us introduce a related multipurpose—or multi-media—approach: integrated industrial waste processing. The concept, in essence, is to combine the best features of on- and off-site waste processing, by symmetry between land development and hazardous waste treatment.

Imagine the construction of a large, modern hazardous waste treatment facility in an industrial area. It is designed to serve the needs of dozens or even hundreds of existing industrial firms or waste generators in that industrial area. These firms are typically too small to economically install their own full range of technologies to neutralize acids, precipitate metals, oxidize organics, and stabilize sludges for ultimate land disposal. Over time, however, if a treatment facility exists, these firms can be induced or required to ship their liquid or semisolid wastes to that treatment center rather than to a landfill. That is the typical model of a free-standing, hazardous waste off-site treatment facility.

Now imagine exactly the same facility, performing the same set of functions, plus an industrial park being developed next to it. This industrial park would target for its customers a new generation of waste generators: electroplaters, foundries, printed circuit board shops, paint factories, whatever. They would locate at the new "integrated industrial processing center" and connect their waste discharge operations directly by special sewer to the hazardous waste treatment facility. What better way to gain the economies of scale for treatment with the flexibility and dynamism of small business operations? What better way to minimize risk to society from hazardous waste management, since the wastes from these new firms "never see the light of day"—never actually enter the ambient environment? What better way to make waste treatment expertise available, essentially on-site, to the smaller waste generator?

Finally, what better way to gain the local community's acceptance for the siting of the very waste treatment facility that lies at the heart of the integrated processing center? Few communities today desire to be the host for a hazardous waste facility, even one designed only for treatment rather than being a "dump." The optics and symbolism and NIMBY politics are very powerful forces. However, suppose they saw at the same time the new taxes, jobs, economic impetus, and positive image for their community associated with the new industrial development to be brought about by the siting of the treatment facility.

A BROADER PERSPECTIVE: GROUNDWATER/
HAZARDOUS WASTE/SURFACE WATER

Traditional thinking and existing environmental statutes force us into modes of action that are too narrow. We pursue individual permitting/ siting approvals and individual cleanup plans, with little relevant concern for and awareness of the broader context of environmental impacts. Environmental impact statements prepared pursuant to the National Environmental Policy Act (NEPA), and state versions, such as California's Environmental Impact Reviews, were supposedly designed to add a cross-media and resources-based perspective to significant land development decisions. Too often, however, they provide instead the procedural basis for endless delay or the structural format for huge lists of peripheral information.

Instead, let us consider a broader perspective on a modern set of environmental management issues—those really at the center of the current national crisis: hazardous waste, groundwater, and surface water. Today, each aspect is being addressed in a series of vacuums:

of policy, of technical and scientific vision, and of leadership. Yet each is an integral component of the broader environmental management and environmental protection web. Thus, fragmented and incomplete decisions under any particular rubric lead to mistakes and failures elsewhere.

Past mismanagement of hazardous wastes has contaminated groundwater. Failure to adopt adequate "remedial actions" around this enormous legacy of the past worsens the situation incrementally, as groundwater moves and gravity pulls downward. Moreover, continuing mismanagement of new hazardous wastes threatens to dwarf even this enormous legacy of past technical and policy-level ineptness.

Superfund may be "Superfailure"; but in this sense RCRA is worse, since the universe of wastes is so much larger. Today's RCRA mistakes and inadequacies are creating more Superfund sites for tomorrow. Even the RCRA perspective is highly focused on a narrow range of risks. Instead, the attention needs to be placed squarely on management— effective, smart, preventive management—of hazardous materials: the chemicals and related materials in use in commerce today. This change would get us out in front of problems, not simply treating or moving around the wastes that come our way by default. Hazardous materials dwarf the waste stream, both in volume and in concentrations. Some solvents are in a billion parts per billion concentration prior to their use (i.e., pure), but we get concerned only when they leak into the groundwater at 8 or 25 or 200 parts per billion.

Effective programs of remedial action and prevention of future leaks—and of hazardous waste source reduction—are essential components of groundwater protection and cleanup. Yet rarely are they viewed today through the same prism. The EPA has its hazardous waste programs, themselves characterized by an overfocus on Superfund rather than RCRA, in its Office of Solid Waste and Emergency Response; yet its groundwater programs rest in the Office of Water. Coordination is attempted; meetings and memos ensue. But an integrated focus on multi-media aspects of hazardous waste and groundwater seems wholly elusive at the federal level.

California has a long-standing and relatively effective program of groundwater management under its Porter-Cologne Water Quality Act. This program is operated under the aegis of the State Water Resources Control Board and nine quasi-independent Regional Water Quality Control Boards that are empowered to make decisions on how best to protect and preserve the "beneficial uses of the surface waters and groundwaters of the state" (California Water Code; California State Water Resources Control Board, 1987). Regional board decisions affect waste discharges and groundwater cleanup, and also underground tanks and surface impoundments.

However, hazardous waste management decisions in California rest with the Department of Health Services' (DHS) Toxic Substances Control Division, as there is no California equivalent of EPA. This unit coordinates with the groundwater regulators, but runs the RCRA and Superfund programs independently. Its focus, naturally, runs to surficial land issues: permits for landfills and hazardous waste treatment, storage, and disposal facilities and cleanups (especially soil removals).

Since mid–1985, the state has been torn by competing proposals for toxics reorganization, embroiled in the politics of the 1986 gubernatorial reelection campaign. Neither the Republican governor's proposals to create a Department of Waste Management nor the Democrats' rejoinders came to grips with the fundamental need to integrate somehow the hazardous waste and groundwater functions into a single pattern of effective action. Indeed, the governor's basic plan would worsen the existing inept situation by shifting the Regional Water Boards' "hazardous waste" functions to the new department—built out of the DHS unit—while leaving groundwater management to those same boards, now completely lacking the resources to do the job.

The third aspect of the dilemma is surface water, always a vital issue of environmental politics in states such as California and throughout the West, and seemingly becoming more important now in much of the East as well. Cleanup of groundwater where it is already contaminated and groundwater protection elsewhere are essential to surface water management level. As noted, effective hazardous waste management is imperative for our groundwater goals to be met.

If we continue to misuse our groundwater resources through allowing further chemical contamination, we will have no choice in the years ahead but to make further demands on surface water supplies. In this regard, the Mono Lake controversy and the Peripheral Canal battle in California—like the Hetch Hetchy drama of years earlier—eventually become intertwined with decisions today on hazardous waste management and groundwater cleanup and/or protection.

California's San Fernando Valley and San Gabriel Valley are both now included on the EPA Superfund NPL; Santa Clara Valley has more proposed NPL sites than any other county in the United States. Groundwater contamination is also widespread in Orange County. These areas need water—and will demand and receive it in the years ahead, from further development of ecologically fragile surface water supplies if no other choices exist. So hazardous waste management and groundwater protection become crucial to the broader context of traditional environmental activism in California: protection of the great Sierras.

Yet, once again, disintegration and fragmentation are the hallmarks of environmental organization. Surface water issues fall under the purview of the Department of the Interior or the Army Corps of Engineers at the federal level, and of the independent Department of Water Resources in the California bureaucracy. Control over drinking water supplies—from both surface water sources and groundwater—rests with a separate unit in EPA under a separate law from hazardous waste or groundwater: the Safe Drinking Water Act. In California, drinking water regulation comes from the Department of Health Services' Sanitary Engineering Branch, totally separate from that department's Toxics Division. If the proposed new Department of Waste Management were created, toxics management would shift there from DHS; but Sanitary Engineering would remain where it is. Fragmentation would increase even more.

In sum, hazardous waste management, groundwater management, and surface water management are three integral components of the same puzzle: modern environmental management. Yet at both federal and California levels—and in many other states—fragmentation ensures the continuing dominance of monomedium myopia despite the public clamor for effective vision and leadership as well as for use of appropriate and timely technological measures.

AN ECOLOGICAL PERSPECTIVE: PROTECTING THE COMMONS THROUGH RISK MANAGEMENT

Garrett Hardin's "Tragedy of the Commons" (1968) teaches us of the need to view environmental policy from a coherent perspective. He argues cogently that the competitive spirit of Adam Smith's free enterprise entrepreneur—so popular in the United States today—can lead only to abject exploitation of common resources. Instead, the solution lies in "mutual coercion, mutually agreed upon."

Our basic generation of modern environmental laws reflects this approach. While their enforcement certainly lags badly behind their rhetoric, the basic principle of coercing ourselves to curb our individual incentives to pollute—transferring our costs on to someone else in space or time—is evident. As noted, we have indeed had much success in achieving the objectives originally articulated by the U.S. Congress and "mutually agreed upon" in our environmental laws.

These laws and this success, however, are focused myopically on single-medium technologies and away from both landuse and cross-media environmental protection. As a result, enforcement of these very environmental laws has exacerbated the underlying industrial hazardous waste crisis associated with the cheap and easy land disposal mentality of a "cowboy economy." For example, an ARCO spokesman has stated that fully 60 percent of all the hazardous wastes generated by his firm's refinery in Carson, California, come from the required air and water pollution control devices (ARCO, 1983).

As the hazardous waste crisis grows daily, the public is clamoring for effective action. Yet both government and industry seem mired in the constraints of the past—including the constraints of today's monomedium statutes. The answer lies in a return to a broader, classical ecological perspective, but with a modern twist: cross-media-environmental management embedded in questions about the true impacts of land development—classic environmental protection rather than relatively much more simplistic end-of-pipe pollution abatement—needs to be combined with a new attention to management of risk from toxics.

In essence, this new cross-media risk management paradigm would have three key components. First, we need to focus on the real risks to people from their environmental exposures: pollutants, exposure pathways, potencies of different chemicals, and individual and aggregate risks. Effective risk assessments—based in sound science but demystified from today's epidemiological jargoneering—can lay the basis for effective risk management.

Second, we need to address our problems comprehensively from a cross-media perspective. Let us not keep shoving the "pollutant of the month" into the dump site of last year, only to have it become the Superfund crisis of next year. This approach may spend money, keep people busy, and give the appearance of progress; but we can and should do better. We need to be able to make socially preferable trade-offs between air and water, between groundwater cleanup and drinking water treatment, and among hazardous waste incineration, NO_x, and offshore oil.

We could take contaminated groundwater at a few parts per billion of TCA—not a known carcinogen—and remove the TCA with carbon filters prior to its use as drinking water. We would then have to chlorinate the water since bacteria grow on the carbon filter. That would create chloroform and other trihalomethanes—known carcinogens—perhaps in concentrations higher than the initial TCA contamination. That would cost money and increase risks to the people drinking the water. While that might be advocated as a technical fix, it would be stupid.

Third, we need to develop a broader set of national standards for toxics—based on the best available science—but then create the forum and procedures for localities to make their own risk management decisions, perhaps choosing to go beyond these national minimum standards toward greater safety but at a local economic price—either in cash or in land development foregone. The beginnings of such an approach are evident in California's Santa Clara Valley, where local elected officials have begun to use the concepts of EPA's Integrated Environmental Management Project to make tough decisions on aquifer management, groundwater cleanup, hazardous waste source reduction, underground tank control, and the ever-present question of "How clean is clean?" EPA national standards and the IEMP methodology of comparing risks from different pollutants, pathways, and sources in a cross-media manner can provide the combination of tools needed for responsible toxics management, in each locality and, in the aggregate, across the country.

In this way, we can indeed "think globally, and act locally" as advocated by René Dubos in pursuit of an acceptable reduction in the risks associated with the tragedy of the toxics commons.

BIBLIOGRAPHY

Ackerman, Bruce A. and William T. Hassler. 1981. *Clean Coal—Dirty Air*. New Haven Conn.: Yale University Press.

Anderson, Elizabeth L. and Carcinogen Assessment Group of the U.S. Environmental Protection Agency. 1984. "Quantitative Approaches in Use to Assess Cancer Risk." *Risk Analysis* 3(4): 277–295.

ARCO. 1983. Personal communication with the author.

California State Water Resources Control Board. 1987. *Preliminary Strategy Groundwater Quality Protection*. Sacramento, November 1987.

California Water Code, Division 7, Section 13241.

Conservation Foundation. 1985. *New Perspectives on Pollution Control: Cross-Media Problems*. Washington, D.C.: The Conservation Foundation.

Hardin, Garrett. 1968. "The Tragedy of the Commons." *Science*, 162: 1243–1248.

Lester, James P. and Ann O'M. Bowman, eds. 1983. *The Politics of Hazardous Waste Management*. Durham, N.C.: Duke University Press.

Mazmanian, Daniel and David Morell. 1988. "The Elusive Pursuit of Toxics Management." *The Public Interest*, No. 90 (Winter 1988): 81–98.

National Research Council. 1983. *Risk Assessment in the Federal Government: Managing the Process*. Washington D.C.: National Academy Press.

Ophuls, William. 1977. *Ecology and the Politics of Scarcity*. San Francisco: W. H. Freeman.

Ottoboni, M. Alice. 1984. *The Dose Makes the Poison—A Plain Language Guide to Toxicology*. Berkeley, Calif.: Vincente Books.

Rodricks, Joseph V. and Robert G. Tardift. 1984. "Conceptual Basis for Risk Assessment." In *Assessment and Management of Chemical Risks*. Washington, D.C.: American Chemical Society.

U.S. Environmental Protection Agency. 1984a. *Risk Assessment and Management: Framework for Decision Making*. EPA 600/9–85–002.

————.1984b. *Uncontrolled Hazardous Waste Site Ranking System: A Users Manual*. U.S. EPA publication no. HW–10 (originally published in the *Federal Register*, July 16, 1982). Washington, D.C.

————. 1986. *Final Report of the Philadelphia Integrated Environmental Management Project*. Regulatory Information Division, Office of Policy Analysis. December.

_____.1988. Weekly Report to the Office of Emergency Response and Re-
    mediation. CERCLIS Data Base. September 2.
U.S. Office of Technology Assessment. 1986. *Superfund Strategy*. Rep. no. ITE–
    317. Washington, D.C.

4

Biotechnology and Thoroughbred Agriculture: More May Be Less

Jack Doyle

ABSTRACT

Advances in biotechnology raise fundamental questions about the role and place of farmers in our agricultural future, about the relative importance of agricultural resources in food and fiber production, about biotechnology's ecological effects, and—most importantly—about who will control the components of agricultural production. Clear evidence exists that biotechnology is making our agricultural system more complex, more expensive, and more vulnerable to disease and disruption. Therefore another key question is whether biotechnology will address these issues as well as the dramatic economic and structural changes it is bringing to the system. Agricultural technology has historically increased productivity by reducing the amount of labor necessary and increasing the amount of land in production. However, with the maturing of biotechnologies we are on the verge of simultaneously being able to dramtically reduce the number of farmers on moderate-sized, family-owned farms and to decrease reliance on traditional land, soil, and water resources. The net effect will be that companies providing agricultural supplies, processing food, and shipping agricultural commodities will increase their control over the terms of production and ultimately over what is produced. Both domestic and international farm supply industries, especially the seed industry, and the agricultural land market are already being markedly altered because of biotechnology; and international political and trade relationships are also potentially vulnerable. Thus as biotechnology advances, the family farm in its best social and ecological form will give way to an impersonal and remote system founded on the commercial utility of science and laws supporting it.

Key Words: agricultural land market, agricultural productivity, bovine growth hormone, effects of biotechnology, family farm, fermentation technologies, genetic engineering, microbial pesticides, patent law, seed industry, structure of agriculture, vulnerability of agricultural system

INTRODUCTION

In Novemter 1985, Texas Tech University announced that a team of scientists who were culturing cotton plant cells in the laboratory discovered that some of those cells had produced cotton fibers. The U.S. Department of Agriculture (USDA), which funded part of this research through a cooperative agreement, was quick to praise the discovery in a report issued a few weeks after the find. "The ability to produce cotton fiber from single cells," said USDA, "presents many new opportunities for scientists."

But what about farmers? USDA and Texas Tech were both careful to point out that laboratory-produced cotton did not necessarily mean that cotton farmers would be displaced. Rather, the university said, these techniques would help move new and improved cotton varieties for cultivation to the farmer more quickly. Yet, the fact remains that cotton was produced in the laboratory without the aid of land or farmers.

Historically, the amount of land used for crop production in the United States has not fluctuated very much over a period of 50 years or more. Yet with biotechnology, yields may rise precipitously in the future, or affect certain substitutions made from fermentation technologies, which could change the land equation dramatically. In some cases, as with certain sweeteners and hydroponic crops, land may not be needed at all. In other cases, as with salt-tolerant and drought-tolerant crops, land not formerly cultivated may be used intensively.

Recently, scientists have also succeeded in producing cocoa butter from cultured cells, and some have speculated on conveyor-belt type factories of the future producing soybean endosperm. In fact, an agriculture without soil or farmers is already with us, at least in part. Weyerhaeuser and Archer-Daniels Midland, for example, are already producing hydroponic lettuce indoors without the help of soil. Kraft, Inc., sponsor of the Disneyworld view of agriculture's future at the Land Pavilion, is now involved with DNA Plant Technology Corporation in making a new line of snack vegetables called Vegisnax, the beginnings of which will be fashioned in the laboratory through a tissue culture and cloning process.

Such advances in biotechnology raise very fundamental questions about the role and place of farmers in our agricultural future, the relative importance of agricultural resources in food and fiber production, and—most importantly—who will have control over the ingredients of agricultural production.

AGRICULTURAL TECHNOLOGY

Historically, the net effect of technology in agriculture has been to reduce the amount of labor necessary to produce a bushel of wheat or a hundredweight of milk. In 1800 it took 373 man-hours to produce 100 bushels of wheat; today it takes less than 9 man-hours to produce the same quantity. In 1960 it took an hour of labor to produce 120 pounds of milk; in 1980, the same hour of labor yielded 480 pounds. With each technological advance in our farm sector, the number of people involved in farming has diminished, while productivity—almost always equated with yield and volume of production—has risen.

On the landscape, with regard to resources, some of our technologies —particularly the mechanical technologies—have been land-expanding technologies in the sense they enabled one man to expand his operation or, in the language of the farmer, "put more land under" that bigger tractor or bigger combine. Indeed, the farmer had to in order to pay for it.

But now, with biotechnology and other technologies in agriculture, we are on the verge of doing three things simultaneously: (1) accelerating the labor-exodus from agriculture like never before; (2) reducing our reliance on the traditional resources of agriculture—land, soil, and water; and (3) lodging more of the "production command" for agriculture in the companies that supply seed, process food, and ship grain.

In the realm of agricultural labor, it is no longer a matter of displacing Mexican-American farm workers with a tomato harvester, although that is still going on, but being able to dramatically eliminate the number of farmers involved in agriculture—especially moderate-size, family-owned farming operations.

According to a recent study by the Congressional Office of Technology Assessment, entitled *Technology, Public Policy, and the Changing Structure of American Agriculture*, biotechnology will figure prominently in changing the demographics of agriculture:

As America enters the era of biotechnology and information technology, agricultural productivity will increase significantly and the structure of agriculture and rural communities will change forever. Approximately 1 million farms will disappear between now and the year 2000, mostly moderate-size and small farms. About 50,000 large farms will then account for 75 percent of U.S. agricultural production.

According to the OTA study, the main beneficiaries of the new technologies will be the operators of large farms:

Operators of small and moderate-size farms, the traditional "backbone of American agriculture," will be less competitive, partly because they will be unable to adopt many of the new technologies. Generally, 70 percent or more of the largest farms are expected to adopt emerging biotechnologies and information technologies, compared to only 40 percent for moderate farms, and about 10 percent for the smallest farms.

Whenever there is technological change and resulting economic flux, there are typically opportunities to consolidate economic advantage, or to be the first in a new market, especially for those already in a strong position. With agricultural biotechnology, companies involved in the selling of agricultural supplies—as well as those processing raw materials and finished products—will measureably increase their control over the terms of production, and ultimately, over what is produced.

In the United States today, roughly 32 percent of all farm sales are under some form of contract or vertical integration. Further, OTA has made two very interesting points about the extent and expansion of contracting: (1) contracting used to be limited to perishable products, but has expanded in recent years to all commodities; and (2) production contracting appears to be associated with commodities where breeding and control of genetic factors play an important role in either productivity determination or quality control.

Given new property rights in the microbial and genetic realms extended to commerce by the U.S. Supreme Court in its 1980 *Diamond* v. *Chakrabarty* decision, the ownership and deployment of the "genes of agriculture" will reside increasingly with commercial entities supplying farm inputs such as seed, breeding stock, chemicals, microbes, and the like, and food processors and grain traders entering contracts with farmers for specific kinds and quantities of crop and livestock products. Yet if this system of agriculture, powered with biotechnology, is solely intent on increasing yield and volume of production, our farmers and our food system may be worse off in the future than they are today.

FEEDING THE THOROUGHBRED

Modern agricultural systems in North America and Europe can be compared to a highly sensitive thoroughbred race horse—high achieving and high performing, but dependent on a special kind of care and attention. In a word, modern agriculture is "high-pedigree" agriculture. It is a highly pampered system of production tended and maintained by all manner of technology, driven to perform at peak levels. It is a system of agriculture built increasingly on hybrid crops and livestock, heavy inputs of fertilizer, water, pesticides, and antibiotics; a system that is capital-, energy-, and technology-intensive. It is, in short, a high-strung system, and as such it is vulnerable to the whims of nature and the "monkey-wrench" factor.

Some scientists and businesspeople, however, have begun to raise questions about the vulnerabilities and costs of this system. William L. Brown, former chairman of the board of Pioneer Hi-Bred International and now chairman of the National Academy of Sciences' Board on Agriculture, has noted that, when our agricultural system is running right, its performance is simply dazzling, "but watch out when something goes wrong."

In 1983 something did go wrong for Midwest corn farmers—something called drought. "Many farmers incurred large economic losses," explained Brown, "because their investment in inputs to support a 150-bushel [per acre] crop withered along with their corn plants."

Brown and others have begun to raise concerns about the volatility of our high-tech, high-yield system. "As we offer the farmer increasingly sophisticated and costly technological packages, we inadvertently exacerbate two related sources of instability in agriculture. High-yield production systems are often more volatile in terms of harvested production, and more erratic in terms of profits for the farmer." In other words, the thoroughbred runs well only when everything clicks.

Because thoroughbred agriculture will increasingly be gene-centered, carrying with it built-in accessory needs for other technologies—and the costs that go with them—biotechnology may make this system more complex, more expensive, and much more vulnerable to disease and disruption than it already is.

SIGNS OF VULNERABILITY

During the last 15 years, U.S. agriculture has witnessed a series of "calamities" that were partly masked because of surplus stocks, crop substitutions, and, in some cases, sheer luck. In 1970–71, the Southern Corn Leaf Blight wiped out 15 percent of the nation's hybrid corn crop, penetrating the Midwest Corn Belt and causing about $1 billion worth of damage. The Mediterranean Fruit Fly continues to pester the citrus and vegetable fields of California and Florida, while the pesticide strategy to deal with this problem has involved elaborate quarantines and even spraying nonfarming regions such as Miami and Menlo Park (California).

More recently, an Avian influenza created havoc in the Mid-Atlantic poultry belt, while a citrus canker damaged Florida's citrus crop, the latter incident resulting in Draconian fire-burning strategies ordered by the government to destroy thousands of seedlings at a number of nurseries. There has also been a continuing string of pesticide incidents—EDB, aldicarb in watermelons, daminozide in apples, and heptachlor in milk—that has shaken consumer confidence in the food system and has caused vested interests to go toe-to-toe with government officials over perceived threats to the public health and safety.

Throughout some of these episodes, we can find real bits of panic, scientific uncertainty, confusion, human error, and perhaps overreaction on the part of both government and vested interests. Yet these incidents drive home the complexity of our food system, with its many moving parts, its vulnerabilities, and its potential volatility in a political and socioeconomic sense.

Today, with biotechnology, we may be moving toward an extension of this high-tech, house-of-cards food system: a system in which one monkey wrench or one unforeseen mutation can create enormous problems. Therefore, a key question about agricultural biotechnology is whether it will simply add newer increments of pedigree improvement to the high-tech, high-yield system now in place—exacerbating its vulnerability, its side effects, and its volatility—or reduce production costs for farmers, broaden the genetic and economic base of agriculture, and reduce the negative environmental and public health side effects.

STABILITY OR VOLATILITY?

Biotechnology will bring unprecedented powers of productivity to agriculture. New genetically engineered crops and livestock products will have the ability to transform agricultural markets swiftly and dramatically, both domestically and internationally. Consider, for example, the recent history and potential impact of applying one new agricultural product from biotechnology called bovine growth hormone.

In late 1979, Genentech, the biotechnology company that was later to become known for breaking a Wall Street record for the sharpest opening price rise of a new stock offering, began work on a substance known as bovine growth hormone, or somatotropin. This hormone is produced naturally in the pituitary of cows and cattle, but only in minute amounts, making isolation and extraction for commercial use prohibitively expensive. But all of that changes with genetic engineering. Genetic engineers have the ability to insert the gene for somatotropin into bacteria that produce the hormone in great quantity as they multiply in fermentation tanks, becoming miniature somatotropin factories. And this is what Genentech had done.

On March 16, 1981, the following story line appeared in the *Wall Street Journal*: "Genentech Reports Output of Hormone to Spur Cow Growth—Joint Venture With Monsanto to Seek Other Varieties For Agriculture Industry." Monsanto and Genentech had, a year earlier, begun a joint research project on "bGH" as it is called, and now the two firms were announcing their intent to commercialize their new product.

"Successful commercialization of bovine-growth hormone could contribute significantly to greater productivity in meat and milk production," explained Genentech's president, Robert A. Swanson. Studies published by Monsanto and other researchers indicate that naturally occurring animal growth hormones can enhance meat production and that dairy cows injected with bovine hormone produced more milk than control animals while consuming the same amount of feed."

Later it was revealed that bGH injected into dairy cows at a rate of about 1/1000th of an ounce per day could raise milk yields as much as 40 percent per cow, but more likely, by 25 to 30 percent per well-managed herd. Such productivity would have formerly taken many generations of selection and breeding utilizing standard techniques.

bGH, of course, is coming into an agricultural sector that is already plagued by overproduction and mounting government surpluses. This situation caused several investigators, including OTA and a few agricultural economists, to look into the new product's potential impact on the dairy sector; and what they found was pretty dramatic. A summary of some of the expected impacts are as follows:

1. There will be rapid and widespread adoption of bGH—90 percent market penetration by 1991–2000; and some surveys in the East and South have indicated that 80 to 90 percent of dairy producers will adopt bGH in the first three years of its availability.

2. On the farm, bGH will effect a 25 percent increase in production and a 26 percent increase in farm returns for those who use it.

3. An increase in the amount of feed concentrate in the feed ration will be required, as the animal's nutrient intake must increase with bGH. Yet the aggregate volume of feed needed industrywide will decrease in proportion to the milk produced.

4. Large dairies will be the earliest adopters, which means market impacts on supply and price will be extremely fast.

5. In the aggregate, as milk production increases in response to bGH, milk prices will fall, reducing the short-term gain in farm returns, as the market seeks a new equilibrium.

6. Within the first three to five years after bGH's introduction, many dairy farmers will find themselves obtaining returns below their fixed operating costs.

7. Milk prices may need to fall 10 to 15 percent.

8. The number of dairy cows nationally may need to be reduced by 30 percent.

9. The number of dairy farms may need to be reduced by 25 to 40 percent.

In addition to these economic impacts of bGH, there are some corollary technological, capital, and management adjustments that may place further economic pressure on small and moderate-size operations. For example, the successful use of bGH requires careful attention to a nutritionally balanced feed ration, and will likely be accompanied by computerized feeding stations that tailor the feed mixture and automated feeding environments that reduce stress on the animal. Such "assisting technologies" will entail capital outlays and continuing operating costs.

Even farmers, normally one of the most pro-technology groups in the United States, have started to balk at the potential economic impacts of bGH. "You bet there's a lot of concern in the industry," said Ivan K. Stickler, a dairy farmer from Iola, Kansas, who is also president of the 11,000-member Mid-America Dairymen, a cooperative based in Springfield, Missouri. Missouri ranks fifth among states in the number of dairy farmers. "This isn't just going to affect dairy farmers," said Stickler of bGH. "It's going to affect all of agriculture, including the businessmen in the farm communities where dairy farmers are going to go out of business."

In May 1986, the Wisconsin Farmers Union, the Wisconsin Milk Marketing Cooperative, and Douglas LaFollette, Wisconsin State Secretary, joined Jeremy Rifkin in a petition to the FDA asking for a delay in the approval and licensing of bGH, calling for a formal environmental impact statement on the new hormone under the National Environmental Policy Act.

Genetically engineered growth hormones are also being targeted for the hog, poultry, and sheep industries, where they could have a similar impact. Overall, biotechnology will dramatically affect the economics of farming, and in so doing will accelerate farm consolidation and farm enlargement. This will mean major structural change in the farming system and considerable instability as the technologies are applied.

FLUX AND INSTABILITY IN THE SEED INDUSTRY

In certain farm-supply industries—most notably the North American and European seed industries—there has already been a dramatic shift in ownership of seed businesses as a result of biotechnology. Hundreds of smaller seed companies have been acquired by chemical, pharmaceutical, energy, agribusiness, and other corporations now speculating on new business opportunities expected to arrive with biotechnology. In the United States alone, more than 140 seed, horticultural, and seed accessory businesses have been acquired by major corporations. Some seed companies have been bought and sold by major corporations two and three times. Many operate as subsidiaries or seed divisions of the parent corporation, and name changes and reorganizations are common. Others, once acquired, are then sold in parts: forage seed to one company, soybean seed to another, and wheat seed to yet another. On a less-pronounced scale, a similar pattern of consolidation and corporate acquisitions has occurred in the livestock genetics business. In the years ahead, biotechnology will likely affect other input industries as well, including the agrichemical, farm equipment, and fertilizer industries.

With biotechnology, there could also be great flux in the agricultural land market. In the absence of other agricultural land uses, biotechnology will have the potential of rapidly releasing farm and ranch land onto the land market, depressing land prices and eroding equity. In the Midwest, we have already seen what can happen to land prices and farmer equity when supply outstrips demand, and the resulting domino effect that hits rural bankers and Main Street businesses. Well, what will happen to land values if rapid "productivity bursts" follow the introduction of bio-technological advances in the wheat sector, or the vegetable sector, and so on?

If bovine growth hormone brings further distress in the Northeast and Great Lakes dairy regions, putting more small dairy farms on the market, what will happen to the land market? In New England there is a booming land market now, but it is not for agriculture. It is for development. We know what has already happened there with the dairy land slated for whole herd buyout. Speculators have been calling dairy farmers several times a week to see when they are going to sell. Once that land is developed, there will be no bringing it back.

INSTABILITY IN THE GRAIN TRADE

Internationally, advances in agricultural biotechnology could also be destabilizing, and could disrupt or completely alter trading patterns, having ramifications for both U.S. agriculture and international politics. At a time when U.S. officials are attempting to place more emphasis on export markets as a means of shifting U.S. agriculture to a more "free market" footing for the purpose of reducing federal outlays for farm programs, advances in biotechnology could make producer nations out of countries that have been U.S. agriculture's valued customers.

If scientists are, for example, successful in genetically engineering crops for increased cold tolerance, huge new markets for crop seed and supporting materials could be created. There are millions of acres in China and Russia where crops are produced only one or two years out of four because of cold. In the United States as well, the northern range of certain crops could be extended through improved cold tolerance. "Think of Russia getting wheat to tolerate freezing," says Ray Valentine of Calgene, Inc., "it would change the geopolitics of the world" Indeed, the repercussions on the international market—and grain exporting countries such as the United States, Australia, and Canada—would be phenomenal.

The Soviets are already pursuing biotechnology with the idea of reducing their dependency on grain imports. According to E. F. Hutton analyst Zsolt Harsanyi, "the USSR is putting a tremendous effort into single-cell protein." By 1990, he claims, the Soviets could be self-sufficient in all animal feed. If they succeed in producing single-cell protein on a large scale," Harsanyi asks, "what impact will that have on our grain export policy?"

Even the introductions of tiny, genetically enhanced microbes in the right places could have very big consequences in terms of trade and international markets. "Much of the soil in the southern hemisphere," explains Ralph Hardy of Biotechnica International, a Boston-based biotechnology company, "suffers from aluminum toxicity which limits phosphate uptake" necessary for plant growth. In this situation, Hardy speculates, biotechnology might produce plants or microbial inoculants that would enable "more effective scavenging of phosphate [by crops] in high aluminum soils." However, such a development, he says, "could make South America an even more significant producer of grains and thereby, a more formidable competitor with U.S. crop agriculture." A similar scenario, explains Hardy, might be proposed for Africa and animal production, "where biotechnology may decrease animal diseases and enable Africa to develop possibly a significant meat packing industry."

In Third World countries, too, the sudden introduction of biotechnological-based agricultural systems could have disruptive and transforming effects for agriculture that would affect both rural and urban populations in those countries, perhaps worsening delicate political and economic situations, and creating instability for years to come.

The problem with all of the potential destabilizing economic and political effects of agricultural biotechnology—both domestically and internationally—is that very few governments or corporations are planning for them. Unless some foresight and planning are brought to bear on the future use of agricultural biotechnology now, capital resources may be wasted, and structural instabilities exacerbated, with farmers, consumers, and Third World nations paying the steepest price.

BIOTECHNOLOGY AND AGRICULTURE'S SIDE EFFECTS

Modern agriculture has made tremendous advances in the science of yield and productivity over the years. But it has also brought with it many undesirable side effects that have had a negative impact on environmental values and public health. In the United States, pesticide and fertilizer runoff and groundwater contamination are serious problems. Nitrates and nitrites from fertilizer runoff have infiltrated some drinking water supplies, posing a health threat, especially to young children. Pesticides, too, are increasingly suspected as carcinogens and mutagens in addition to their well-known deleterious effects on beneficial insects and wildlife.

Will biotechnology make agriculture more environmentally compatible than it is today? Will it help reduce or eliminate negative environmental and public health side-effects? Will it be more ecologically responsible than what has gone before it?

In theory, biotechnology ought to help agriculture reduce its side effects and be more environmentally acceptable. In the long run, nitrogen-fixing cereal crops may eliminate the need for a great deal of nitrogen fertilizers, and improved nitrogen-fixing microbes that are already nearing the market can reduce the use of fertilizer by improving its efficiency. New crop varieties and livestock breeds that genetically resist disease pathogens and insect attack can reduce or eliminate the need for pesticides. Indeed, with a more knowledgeable practice of genetics, crops and livestock could incorporate "built-in" resistance traits for disease pathogens and insect pests that might make the use of chemical insecticides obsolete. Some biotechnologists even talk boldly of making crops "immune" to disease and insects.

Yet in the short run of commercial reality, we may see biotechnology being used to extend the pesticide era rather than end it. At least 25 companies now have some investment in using biotechnology to make crop strains of corn, soybeans, cotton, and others genetically resistant to the ill effects of herbicides. This could be useful, because herbicides are sometimes lethal to the crop as well as the weeds. Other companies are exploring ways that chemical plant growth regulators can be used in syncrony with genetically engineered crop strains to maximize some desired effect, be that related to mechanical harvesting, early planting, uniform ripening, shelf life, or other characteristic. Given the EPA's recent scrutiny of several herbicides and at least one plant growth regulator for potential carcinogenicity, these biotechnological research thrusts should be approached with considerable concern.

MICROBIAL PESTICIDES AND NEW ECOLOGICAL RISKS

Some companies, however, have begun to prepare for the future and are pursuing biotechnology for ways to develop new biological pesticides that may one day replace chemical pesticides. Research and commerce are here engaged in the task of working with nature to a certain extent rather than against her.

Historically, the net effect of modern agriculture has been to disturb and replace complex ecological systems with relatively simplified agricultural environments. Modern agriculture—in its brute-force conquest and reshaping of the environment—has helped give rise to the very plagues that haunt it and make certain the use of pesticides, antibiotics, and all manner of mechanical and other supplements aimed at protecting those man-made environments.

Now, however, with molecular biology we may have a chance to better understand the ecological underpinnings of agriculture, and make that system work to the advantage of sustained productivity and a better rate of return for farmers who now spend too much time and money fighting it with pesticides and machinery. However, if biotechnology is used to create only biological facsimilies of existing chemical and mechanical products and approaches in dealing with nature, then we will succeed only in repeating our past mistakes, but this time in a more irreparable manner.

For example, genetically engineering microbes with multiple toxin genes—to do what broad-spectrum chemical pesticides now do—may invite ecological havoc. We know very little about soil microbes, over 80 percent of which have never been cultured in the laboratory, and as many as 90 percent of which do not even have names. Adding toxin genes to this realm in the form of "multiple warhead" microbes aimed at killing one or more kinds of insect or fungi is really playing ecological roulette.

Biotechnology will present risks to both the economy and the environment because of what we do not know about the organisms being released, and the environments into which they will be released. The ability to predict what might happen with genetically engineered organisms will have to build upon what is known about the ecology of existing organisms. But the trouble is, we have not collected much ecological information on existing organisms.

Today, in the agricultural environment, there are—and these figures may be low—at least 160 species of bacteria, 250 kinds of viruses, 8,000 species of insects, and 2,000 species of weeds. But how much do we really know about these and other unidentified species? Many ecologists agree that little is known about the dynamics of how organisms such as these establish themselves, or why some species multiply in nature and others do not, or what attributes make some organisms good at dissemination and others poor.

Yet it is not surprising to find that we lack such data and predictive capabilities. Only since 1983 have our government and scientific institutions begun to think in-depth about what genetically altered organisms might do in the real-world environment outside the laboratory. Prior to this time, the real focus of biotechnology and gene-splicing was inside the laboratory.

Only as recently as June 1985 did molecular biologists and ecologists, meeting for the first time, begin to start a scientific dialogue on the issue of environmental release. In Philadelphia in the summer of 1986, meeting under the auspices of the American Society for Microbiology and other organizations, they met under the title of "Engineered Organisms in the Environment: Scientific Issues." Not a whole lot of agreement was reached at that meeting, but it did serve to stimulate more involvement in this question from ecologists. However, one thing is clear: as more and more ecologists have been drawn into this debate in recent years, more and more questions have begun to be asked that were not being asked before, and more and more uncertainty and data gaps have begun to appear.

SHIFT IN PROPERTY RIGHTS AND LOSS IN SOCIAL VALUE

Finally, there is the matter of property rights—what is owned and can be owned, what responsibilities flow from certain kinds of ownership, and what the relationship with natural resource property, for example, teaches us as individuals as well as a larger society.

Since 1980 we have seen a dramatic change in property rights as that concept affects biology and certain food-producing resources. The Supreme Court's *Diamond* v. *Chakrabarty* decision opened the doors to the patenting of man-made microbes and individual genes. True, seed-propagated plants and asexually propagated plants have been eligible for patenting since 1970 and 1980, respectively, but much of the world has not yet entered these new legal realms of property rights, within the larger arena that is often called "intellectual property."

There are some commercial interests in Europe now that are arguing that a privately owned gene used in ten different soybean varieties should, in effect, extend that owner's interest in those ten varieties. Here in the United States, the pharmaceutical industry has been successful in obtaining a law for longer patent terms in trade for quicker generic drug approval, which most of the major drug firms now also sell. In 1986 the U.S. Senate considered a bill that would similarly extend the patent term for pesticides, veterinary, and biotech products (and processes) used in agriculture.

Aside from the questions of patenting's impact on monopolization and rates of innovation—which in agriculture may well have a bearing on the farmer's cost of production and the availability of more benign environmental alternatives—the upshot of all of this patent law, I believe, will be to change how people think about property, and the responsibility that comes with certain kinds of property.

CLOSURE

We often hear that "the family farm" is anachronistic in this modern age, and we are witnessing its demise in our lifetime. But the family farm is a special economic entity when it comes to property, the meaning of ownership, and the responsibility of ownership. In its best social and ecological form, the family farm is stewardship and reciprocal economic responsibility wrapped up into one desirable, locally participating entity—all founded on a piece of property.

However, we are losing the opportunity for those living lessons in ownership responsibility, environmental give-and-take, and beneficial production for society. We are moving away from live-on-the-land agriculture and the values that come with it, and away from a more human-scale property right to a more impersonal and remote property right founded on the commercial utility of science and laws drawn to accommodate that world view. As a society, I think that is unfortunate, because it will make us more competitive and exploitive in the full negative sense of those terms—but also less accountable and somewhat less human. And from René Dubos' perspective, that was surely not what he had hoped for.

5

Maintaining Agricultural Land as the Petroleum Era Passes

R. Neil Sampson

ABSTRACT

As the world works its way through the remaining decades of readily available petroleum fuels, many major technological transformations will be needed. One of the most critical to human welfare will be the transformation of agriculture, which in the developed countries has become totally dependent on petroleum and its products. Finding new technologies to replace the petroleum-fueled technologies upon which agriculture now depends should not prove impossible, but it could be exceptionally expensive and disruptive if the essential research directions are not established soon, while time for experimentation and adjustment remains.

Key Words: agriculture, agricultural economics, land use, low-input agriculture, petroleum, soil conservation, technology

A TRANSITION LOOMS

The maintenance of a productive agriculture is central to the prosperity of the United States, and petroleum is the key ingredient in modern agricultural technology. The world has been experiencing wide fluctuations in the price of petroleum and its products, and public opinion about petroleum availability for the future swings with these cycles. But the simple fact remains: oil is a nonrenewable resource. Even with massive supplies still available, it should be clear that the twentieth century will, indeed, be remembered by future historians as the "Oil Age." By some time early in the next century, we will no longer be able to rely on the cheap, plentiful supplies of petroleum that fuel today's technology.

To agricultural producers, scientists, industries, and policy makers, the passage of the Oil Age means that a new agricultural technology must emerge. We cannot predict for certain when it will be needed, or exactly what it will entail, but there are several things that we can predict with some assurance. First, it will be easier for all concerned if the transition is started well before it becomes essential. Waiting until agriculture is under stress from inevitably rising costs of production will make new technologies both more difficult and more expensive to develop.

Second, the new technologies must be profitable to agricultural producers. The current wave of farm bankruptcies is more than a minor shake-out of inefficient operators. It is a widespread economic and technological failure in the system, which has developed in ways that leave the basic producers open to financial shocks that many cannot absorb. In other words, no matter how agriculture changes in the future—whether there are 2 million farmers or 200,000—the production technologies used must be profitable to those producers.

Finally, the new technologies must be more harmonious with the ecological realities of the land. Current production methods are degrading the natural resources of the United States, and that cannot continue indefinitely. Those natural resources are part of the fixed asset capital of the nation. They produce goods, services, and jobs that are essential to our welfare. Like any other asset, they can be depreciated and their productivity depleted. They can, for all practical purposes, wear out if not maintained properly (Nothdurft, 1984). The declines in soil quality, forests, rangelands, and watersheds that have accompanied current agricultural technologies and economic trends can be halted and even reversed, but only if the proper directions are taken as post-petroleum agricultural technology emerges.

Can these goals be achieved? Can we design a new technology that relies less on oil, is more profitable for producers, and maintains natural resource productivity? My answer is "Yes, we can, if we decide to do it and start soon." Those goals are not incompatible with each other and may, in fact, be interrelated and self-reinforcing. But time is important, and it will not be easy to convince leaders and policy makers that it is time to begin. For many who have grown comfortable with what we do today, or whose current businesses prosper by selling the products of the Oil Age, the next technology may sound threatening. For those who insist on clinging to today's products until the bitter end, it almost certainly will be.

We must begin the process today. New and exciting technologies are already in view. Many are so unprecedented that we have little or no idea where they may lead. Biotechnology, for example, may provide us with entirely new varieties of plants and animals that have been "genetically engineered" in ways that will revolutionize production. Just how that "engineering" is directed is of vital importance.

For the past four decades, new plant varieties have been designed mainly as more efficient pipelines to channel an ever-increasing flow of petroleum subsidies into agriculture. New varieties won favor because they made better use of fertilizer, were more tolerant of chemical weed-killers, or more resistant to ever-evolving strains of disease organisms. That this trend reinforced a "technology treadmill," pushing farmers toward more and more crop specialization, higher and higher on-farm costs, and greater vulnerability to both environmental and economic disruption was of little concern so long as there were ample supplies of petroleum and its products at low prices.

Now, however, that has changed, and it will change much more in the coming decades. We now will need varieties that are more efficient pipelines of the basic growth factors in the agricultural ecosystem. We will need plants that utilize sunlight, water, and carbon dioxide more efficiently. We will adopt plants that utilize soil nutrients well, or that contribute to biological nutrient cycling and soil-building. We will value plants that produce from the same rootstock year after year, to cut management costs and provide year-round protection of topsoil and nutrients.

In other words, we will continue to act in an economically rational fashion. When petroleum and its products were plentiful and cheap, we used them to replace limited land and expensive labor. As petroleum grows more dear, we will replace its products with those that are more abundant and less costly. That is no insurmountable technological challenge, it demands only that we understand what we must do, and begin to do it.

To make this case, we will examine the extent to which agriculture depends on oil and its products, and on the current situation and probable future course in petroleum supplies. The impact of recent agricultural trends, both on the financial stability of producers and the ecological stability of the land, will be examined. We will then turn to the future, suggesting directions for research and development that cannot only ease the inevitable transition away from reliance on oil, but also improve both the financial and ecological performance of agricultural technology.

AN OIL-BASED AGRICULTURE

We hear a great deal about the virtues of "modern" agriculture and its unparalleled rise in productivity and output since 1940. Yields have risen dramatically, but not as fast as energy inputs have climbed. A close examination reveals that our progress in recent years has been closely tied to an ever-increasing flow of fossil fuels into the production system. Take away those fuels, and all the tractors, irrigation pumps, fertilizers, pesticides, crop dryers, and other apparatuses that they drive, and agriculture would be back to its turn-of-the-century status.

One indicator of the importance of petroleum to current productivity is seen in Figure 5.1, which is taken from U.S. Department of Agriculture statistical bulletins. The dramatic rise in the farm output index that began around 1940 is plainly evident. This has been accompanied, as the figure shows, by only a very slight rise in cropland acres. What has risen, and dramatically, is the amount of purchased inputs, particularly agricultural chemicals, machinery, and such things as feed and seed. Figure 5.2 shows these trends.

Two problems have emerged as a result of this vastly increased use of purchased inputs. First, the energy efficiency of agricultural production appears to have been falling since the early 1970s. Farmers increased their energy use from 6.3 percent of national consumption in 1967 to 7.1 percent in 1981, but Figure 5.3 indicates that each added unit of energy in 1980 resulted in some 20 percent less output than it would have a few years earlier. Second, prices skyrocketed as a result of the Arab oil embargoes of 1973 and 1979, with the major rise coming after 1979 (See Figure 5.4).

THE IMPACT ON FARMERS AND FARM COMMUNITIES

This "double whammy" has agricultural producers reeling. Farmers today spend nearly two-thirds of their cash receipts to buy inputs. In 1983, for example, that amounted to $18 billion for feed, $7.4 billion for fertilizer, $4 billion for seed, $9.8 billion for machinery, and $15.8 billion for fuel and machinery maintenance (Doyle, 1985). This has been particularly difficult for those who lack cash reserves and must borrow money to cover annual operating costs, because interest rates more than doubled during the same period (USDA, 1988). Interest payments now amount to as much as 30 percent of total farm expenses, that percentage having doubled between 1970 and 1982 (Leman and Paarlberg, 1988).

Not too surprisingly, one result of these trends has been a flood of farm failures, accompanied by declining rural economies and communities. In 1984, USDA estimated that some 10 percent of all farmers were facing debt-to-asset ratios that could put them out of business within two years unless the situation did not improve (Cook and Sechler, 1985). Off-farm jobs, as well, are drying up at precisely the time desperate farm families need them most, according to Dan Levitas of

Figure 5.1
Farm Output Index and Total Cropland, 1910–80

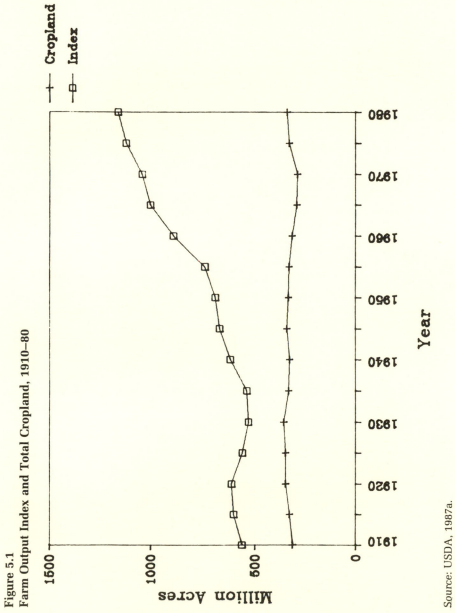

Source: USDA, 1987a.

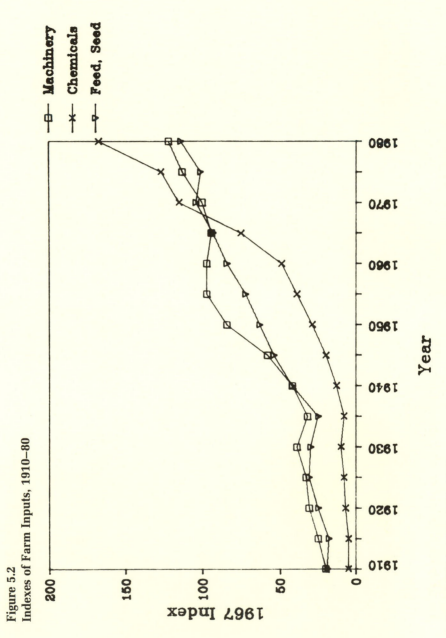

Figure 5.2
Indexes of Farm Inputs, 1910–80

Source: USDA, 1980, 1983, 1987a.

Figure 5.3
Energy Productivity Index, 1967–80

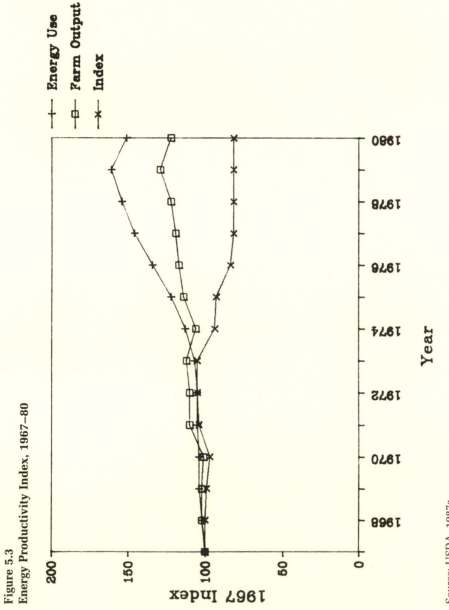

Source: USDA, 1987a.

67

Figure 5.4
Energy Price Index, 1967–82

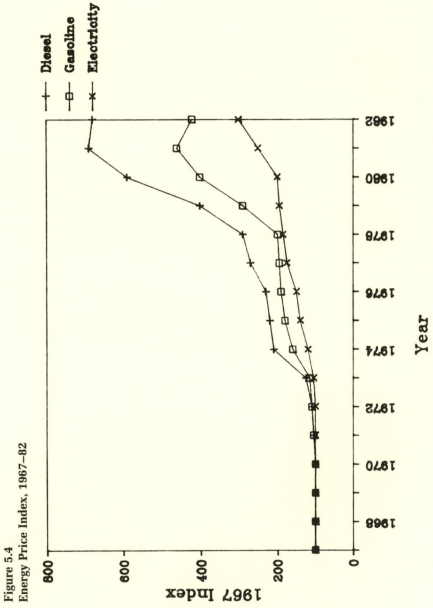

Source: USDA, 1983.

Rural America. "On the average," Levitas estimates, "one business serving a rural community folds for every seven farms that go under" (quoted in Wessel, 1983).

One of the oft-touted "solutions" to the farm crisis of the 1980s is to increase exports of farm commodities. This was, however, the "solution" of the 1970s as well, and its record is not all that good. Farmers were told that the world was awaiting their bounty, and they increased the acreage of corn, soybeans, and wheat—the major export crops—by some 30 percent between 1972 and 1982. The acres devoted to exports jumped to nearly 40 percent of all planted acres. By 1981 the net trade balance for agriculture had risen to $26.5 billion and was the one bright spot in the U.S. trading performance.

That performance was short-lived, however, and the fall came quickly. Around the world, inflation caused by the 1979 oil price jump stopped growth in its tracks, dampening demand for imports. In many countries, rising interest rates created a debt crisis that demanded a cutback in imported products of all kinds, including food and feed. The value of the U.S. dollar rose in relation to other currencies, making food from the United States a particularly expensive luxury, which many countries could avoid. Large crops, including outstanding performance in many countries that formerly had been unable to meet their needs, further dampened world demand.

American farmers, despite the fact that export markets diminished significantly, still did not do too badly in terms of competition. Analysts Kenneth Cook and Susan Sechler (1985) point out that 1984 grain exports were 20 percent above the 1972–79 average. In other words, while we have dropped down from the 1981 peak, we are still doing better than our historical average, both in terms of actual exports and market share in the major export crops. What has suffered has been our expectations, more than our performance. We thought the boom would last forever, and it did not.

If the truth were told, the boom was not all that great. Not for farmers, at any rate. Net farm income dropped more than half—in constant-dollar terms—from its 1973 peak, and it displayed erratic behavior throughout the big export expansion years. Between 1978 and 1980, with exports rising from around $28 billion to some $40 billion, net farm income sank 40 percent (Wessel, 1983). It got so bad in 1983 that the federal payments associated with the Payment-in-Kind (PIK) program made up over half of all net farm income, which had dropped by half between 1981 and 1983! To add to those woes, land values had declined sharply from the inflation-pushed values of the 1970s, and many farmers saw their total asset value drop by one-third to one-half.

As a result, the end of a decade of historic export expansion found the farm economy in total disarray. Those farmers still managing to hang onto their holding—particularly those in the beleaguered "middle-sized" family-owned and family-operated class—can ill afford another decade of "prosperity" such as the one they have just experienced.

Exports, while being a marvelous way to reduce built-up inventories and earn additional dollars for commodities that might otherwise go unsold, are a highly volatile, seldom profitable, and totally unpredictable basis upon which to build a national production strategy. Forcing farmers, already producing for prices that fail to meet the oil-driven production costs they face, to accept prices at even lower levels in order to compete for an even-larger share of that volatile and unprofitable world market is a prescription for disaster.

IMPACT ON THE LAND

The growth of high-technology agriculture in recent decades has been accompanied by significant damage to land resources, although the data to document both the extent of that damage and its significance are incomplete and, at times, conflicting.

Changes in natural resource systems take place slowly, and are seldom noticeable in periods of less than a decade. Unfortunately, good data on soil productivity, erosion rates, and so on, do not exist prior to the late 1970s. At that time, in response to growing concern for the treatment of U.S. farmlands as the export boom intensified crop production, the Soil Conservation Service conducted the 1977 National Resources Inventory (NRI) (USDA, 1982). This effort, the first to demonstrate erosion's extent in a scientifically defensible way, still fell far short of meeting all expectations. An improved version of the NRI was conducted in 1982, which generally corroborated most of the 1977 data and showed, as might be expected, little fundamental change in the five-year period (USDA, 1987b).

What we do not know, however, is how these soil conditions relate to the conditions found, say, in the 1930s, when national concern for soil erosion and land damage was triggered by the Dust Bowl. Surveys and estimates done in that era, which some analysts have attempted to compare to modern conditions, simply are not comparable. Thus we need to look at today's conditions and judge them for what they are, and how they meet our expectations for a sustainable, profitable agriculture.

In 1982, according to the NRI data, U.S. farmers used some 421 million acres for cropland. Of that land, some 96.8 million acres—almost one in every four—were suffering topsoil loss at rates that were more than double what could be replaced through normal soil-building processes (USDA, 1987b). In other words, almost one acre in four was deteriorating. That deterioration, while often taking several years, if not

decades, to affect production visibly, is not so important for its magnitude as for its direction. No society can sustain itself permanently by
destroying the resource base that sustains it. Building a sustainable
future means finding ways to stabilize, if not improve, the productivity
of the land and its associated natural resources.

It is not that real economic costs do not exist, but they are hard to
quantify. According to the EPA (1989), farms deliver over half of the
phosphorous, nitrogen, and sediment loadings that pollute the nation's
waters. Agronomist James Bauder (1984) of Montana State University
estimates that farm losses of nitrogen, phosphorous, and potassium due
to erosion add up to $1.1 billion a year. Thus, significant amounts of
the fertility elements purchased by farmers end up washing into public
waters, where they promote the growth of algae and other undesirable
plants that can contribute to fish kills and other water quality problems.
One person's asset becomes another's nuisance, and costs are incurred
twice.

The impact of soil erosion on crop yields has been a much-studied
topic in recent years, but the results are still difficult to generalize for
the nation as a whole. Agronomists George W. Langdale and William
Schrader (1982), for example, compared the results of eight studies
conducted between 1961 and 1977. Yield reductions due to the removal
of all topsoil ranged from 8 to 30 percent for corn, 20 to 40 percent for
soybeans, 12 to 20 percent for cotton, and 11 to 24 percent for small
grains. A two-year field study in Georgia indicated that severe erosion
can cut soybean yields by 50 percent (USDA, 1985). What these and
other studies show is that not only are erosion rates highly variable,
their impact on crop yields varies widely from soil to soil. In general,
soils that are deep to a restrictive layer that would inhibit root growth
or water penetration show less plant growth impact from erosion damage than do shallower soils where a small loss of topsoil may cause
fairly quick and visible reductions in productivity.

What are the costs to society of allowing current rates of soil erosion
to proceed? Researchers William E. Larson, Frank J. Pierce, and Robert
H. Dowdy (1983) have recently estimated that the on-farm costs would
be fairly modest—reducing national crop yields somewhere in the range
of 10 percent over the next 100 years—provided that today's farming
technology can be sustained and low-price fertilizers are available to
replace lost nutrients. That proviso may be more important than past
history would indicate, as we shall soon explore.

The off-farm costs must be added to this loss estimate, and while it
is not easy to estimate the amount of damage caused by eroding soils,
many analysts believe that off-farm damages far exceed the on-farm
losses. Analysts Edwin H. Clark, Jennifer Haverkamp, and William
Chapman (1985), in a recent study published by The Conservation

Foundation, estimated that erosion from U.S. croplands costs the nation $2.2 billion annually in water quality damage alone.

What we can say with fair assurance about the soil erosion losses being sustained by U.S. farmlands is that they are likely to continue—and may accelerate—unless significant changes are made. While it is argued that farmers might be expected to manage land for long-term productivity, the reality is that they must live in the present. What is true in the present is that soil conservation is irrelevant to the business of farming. Market forces do not reward—and often penalize—the conservation farmer (Sampson, 1981). Until passage of the 1985 Farm Bill—to what effect we will not know for several years—all USDA programs were available to all farmers, no matter whether or not they abused the land.

In the meantime, investments in soil and water conservation improvements are not being maintained. USDA economist George A. Pavelis (1983) has shown that there was rapid growth in investment in conservation measures between 1935 and 1955, but the last three decades have been marked with a consistent decline, in which depreciation has outpaced new investment. During that same period, public spending for conservation programs, in real dollar terms, has also declined. Neither farmers nor governments, when facing imminent financial travail, opt for investments in the long-term future, no matter how rational such investments might seem to the outside observer.

LOOKING AHEAD FOUR DECADES

The point has been made that today's agriculture is heavily dependent on petroleum and its products. Neither the economic damage to farmers nor the ecological damage to the land would present an insurmountable problem if the real cost of yield-improving inputs and technologies were to continue to drop as it has for the past 100 years. But how likely is that? Far too unlikely, I would argue, to be a good basis for a policy strategy. For one thing, we are simply not going to be able to depend on oil to fuel our productivity growth in the next 40 years the way it did in the last four decades.

Petroleum is not, of course, in imminent danger of disappearing, and the agricultural technologies that flow from it will be around for many years. But it is equally clear that petroleum is not an inexhaustible resource, that costs associated with it will inexorably rise, and that agriculture must find another "anchor" upon which to build productivity.

In 1956 a geologist for Shell Oil, M. King Hubbert, developed an estimate of U.S. oil reserves and a method to predict their rate of exploitation. While his methods have been argued, refined, and adjusted, they have also been fairly well borne out by actual experience. Hubbert predicted that U.S. oil production would peak somewhere around 1970 and that, by 2020, domestic soil supplies will be largely depleted. Other studies, including those that assess the impact of Alaskan oil and other, more recent trends basically corroborate Hubbert's projections (Gever, et al., 1986).

For the world as a whole, the picture is little different. Hubbert predicts that world oil production will peak in the mid–1990s, then drop sharply in the first decades of the next century (Nothdurft, 1984). This decline could be altered, of course, depending on the reaction of people to the price increases that will inevitably accompany declining supplies.

Over the past decade, we have heard much rhetoric about the fact that our oil woes were the fault of government controls—or pricing systems. While both were no doubt contributing to the short-term situation, it is misleading to think that either will affect the ultimate outcome greatly.

Look at the impact of price, for example. U.S. oil production was 10 percent less in 1982 than in 1970, despite the fact that 1982 prices were $33 a barrel as compared to $3 (Yergin, 1982). Our problem was not one of demand or price, it was one of supply. We have exploited our major stocks; future supplies will be harder and more expensive to find; and we will finally face the ultimate problem: When the energy costs of finding and developing an oil field exceed the energy benefits it can provide, that oil will stay in the ground. It will also, it should be pointed out, stay in oil shale, tar sands, coal deposits, and dozens of other places that have been variously touted to be "bonanzas" in recent years, awaiting only until "oil prices rise to levels where this technology will be profitable."

The paradox of energy is that exploring for and developing new energy sources is an energy-intensive business, and as supplies get deeper, further from civilization, more difficult to find, or more thinly dispersed through the rock and soil that contain them, the amount of energy needed to develop them rises accordingly. The same price level that might send a company scurrying to find a new source will also drive its cost structure.

The situation is analogous to the carrot dangling from the stick tied to the neck of the donkey. No matter how fast the donkey moves, he never gains on the carrot. Those who argue that price increases will draw forth new energy resources at lower prices must demonstrate how, through some technological breakthrough, it is feasible to alter dramatically the energy in-energy out equation. Otherwise, they are simply proposing that the donkey run faster.

We are thus forced to conclude that the dramatic expansion of petroleum-derived inputs that has accompanied the historical explosion of agricultural productivity in the last four decades will not be repeatable in the next 40 years. This is not to say that agricultural productivity itself cannot continue to rise, perhaps as fast or faster than before. What it says is that we must find a new fuel to drive that technological advance, and we must find it fairly soon.

PLANNING THE TRANSITION

Perhaps the most challenging task facing Americans as they set about to develop a new agricultural technology to replace the oil-based one we have grown so dependent upon is that there is no apparent reason to do it. As oil prices slid toward $15 a barrel in the mid–1980s, politicians were quick to note how great those price declines would be for U.S. business and industry, and how they would herald a new era of economic growth.

That really never came to pass, and it was certainly never noted in Midland, Texas, where the number of active oil rigs and solvent drillers diminished daily through those supposed "boom times" (Maraniss, 1986). It was also not felt in Anchorage, where state revenues had become dependent on oil prices. More importantly, perhaps, the 1980s market glut helped devastate economies in places such as Mexico and Venezuela, where oil revenues are about all there is to stave off economic collapse.

What happened, to be sure, is that the oil glut cut exploration, reduced incentives for improving energy efficiency in homes and businesses, and killed the search for alternative sources of energy. In the long run, however, the most threatened aspect of the economy may be agriculture, where the "crisis of abundance" has prevented us from seriously addressing the need for research into a less-oil-dependent future.

The critical aspect here is the public and private policies that guide the development of new agricultural technologies for the post-Oil Age. Those technologies will, in a large way, determine whether or not the nation prospers in the twenty-first century, or whether we are forced— as are many nations in the world today—to subsist on a resource base so badly damaged as to prevent the maintenance of a healthy society.

AGRICULTURE IN THE POST-OIL AGE

One of the first questions to face is "How can U.S. agriculture survive if its major source of energy dries up?" The answer, of course, is that agriculture has been around for 10,000 years, of which only the past 40 have been petroleum-based. We have done exceptionally well in using this one-time bounty of nature, but we can also learn to do without it. That transition may not be pleasant, but it is possible. There are several strategic directions that can be taken that will, at the least, ease the transition and could, with luck, be the door-opener to new eras of prosperity and productivity that equal or exceed any we have seen. Without a crystal ball to see the ultimate outcomes, we could at least suggest what some of these directions might be.

Break the Debt Treadmill

This may be more than a matter of agricultural policy. It is national macroeconomics that must change here, and farmers have very limited clout to address these issues (Leman and Paarlberg, 1988). But getting the federal deficit under control, maintaining reasonable interest rates, and stabilizing the dollar at rates more comparable to other currencies is not just a goal of agriculture.

The problems afflicting farmers today—high and rising costs plus low or nonexistent profits—face the forest-products industry, mining, fishing, and virtually every other basic industry in the United States. The political and economic system has, in recent years, rewarded those who took their investments abroad and built up debt rather than productive assets in the United States. Wider recognition of this among the affected constituencies may result in a political consensus to alter the directions in which the nation is currently headed.

One thing is for certain: we can lose 10 percent of the remaining farmers without making much of a blip on the national macroeconomic picture. But there are a lot of rural communities that will essentially cease to function if that happens there. There are state and regional economies where such a disaster, and its resultant side effects, is equally unthinkable. So we must address the debt treadmill upon which U.S. farmers find themselves today and break it with the fewest possible casualties. Part of that must be addressed by national policies affecting foreign exchange, credit, insurance, and income supplements. Much of it, however, will be cured only by a hard look at farm production technology.

Low-Input Agriculture

It is said that conservation tillage is the fastest-growing agricultural technology in history. Former Secretary of Agriculture John Block (1984) put his finger on the reason. "Conservation tillage saves soil, toil, and oil," Block told participants at a 1984 conference on the subject. In other words, less tillage means less cost; and if you can do it while maintaining yields, that translates into more profits. The soil savings are great, and most farmers see them as a very important aspect of conservation tillage, but what drives adoption of the new methods is the promise of higher profits.

Conservation tillage may well point the way toward further refinement of classical production techniques as well. Take weed control, for example. For decades now, farmers have attempted—in vain—to eradicate the plants that compete with their crops for sunlight, moisture, and nutrients. Moving from the sterile, clean, narrow monocultures that marked that attempt to the messier, more complex ecosystems that characterize conservation tillage may help farmers find a way to manage weeds as part of the growth system.

Under this strategy, weeds would be tolerated so long as they remain below a damaging threshold. Certain plants, while not economically salable, may have value in nutrient recycling, topsoil protection, or as the host to beneficial organisms that prey on crop-damaging pests. Such plants,while they compete for space with crop plants, could be tolerated so long as their benefits exceeded their damage.

Similarly, integrated pest management, which has been growing in favor and sophistication for several years, is an attempt to encourage a broader, more diverse mix of organisms in the cropping system. In many cases, the broader mix of species will have a self-controlling effect; and the farmer, by recognizing that he can tolerate a little crop damage better than a big pesticide expense, saves his pesticides for those outbreaks that threaten to get away and destroy the delicate balance in the field. A short step beyond these techniques is the return to crop rotations and sod crops that can break up disease and pest cycles, aid in nutrient recycling, rebuild topsoil, and support higher yields with less need for purchased inputs.

Old-fashioned? Perhaps, but not necessarily. An integrated crop, soil, species, and water management system—if it is to be a high producer—must be very intensively managed. It will demand that farmers be much more technically sophisticated, not less. It may not simply save oil, it may replace oil with information. As Robert Wetherbee (1984), a Minnesota farmer and conservation leader, says, "using conservation tillage has meant that I need to be more aware of what is involved in my farming operation. Conservation tillage has meant an increase in awareness and knowledge by me as a farmer." Not too surprisingly, Wetherbee was an early adopter of farm computer technology—one more way to replace brute strength and purchased horsepower with managed information.

So one of the ways to slip out of the oil trap is to manage better, and make plants and animals do for free what was formerly only achievable with chemicals purchased in a bag or can. That kind of low-input agriculture—whether it is called conservation tillage, organic farming, or whatever—offers many options for the post-Oil Age, and research

into better low-input methods deserves strong support and encourage-
ment from agricultural policy makers and leaders.

One of the problems in low-input agriculture will be for agribusiness
to find a profitable role in it. If farmers buy less, business sells less,
and there are few businesses where lower sales mean higher profits, so
that is a problem. The answer, of course, is that business will have to
change what it manufactures and sells, in keeping with the technological shifts in agriculture.

Richard H. Foell (1984) of Chevron Chemical Company points out
that this has always been the case. "From the first colonial blacksmiths
to today's multi-national corporations . . . from Whitney's cotton gin and
McCormick's reaper to today's sophisticated equipment and chemicals
. . . the inventor and the businessman have marched side by side with
the farmer toward better crops, less labor and high yields," he notes.
It has been, and will be, the challenge of business to continue to an-
ticipate what farmers will need, develop it, and sell it for a competitive
price. In the process, some of today's products will go the way of
yesterday's harnesses and buggy whips. Whether or not a company
follows such a product into oblivion will be up to that company and
the foresight of its leaders.

Incentives for Investment in Productivity

In the United States, most of the land used for agriculture is privately
held, and most of the investments in future productivity must necessarily come from private investors and owners. But that should not be
misinterpreted to indicate that there is no role for government to play.

Government, by its nature, is the only institution that can control the
climate of economic incentives that will encourage private investments
in long-term natural resource productivity. Markets and prices will not
offer such incentives, because markets and prices are relevant only to
transactions between individuals. Investment in natural resource
strength is a transaction between people and the earth and, as such, is
not measured by dollars or bartered in markets.

When a farmer grows corn, but does not protect the topsoil from
washing away, the market pays no attention whatsoever. The corn goes
for the same price as that of the farmer who spends additional effort
to protect the topsoil. When a forest owner cuts down a forest, but fails
to plant a new one, that failure is of no consequence to the sawmill,
or to any of the end users of the wood or paper products that flow from
the forest.

In the forest example, the many years involved in forest growth and
the high costs and risks needed to bring a forest from seedling to sawlog
have caused every country in the Western world to provide special tax

incentives to encourage reforestation and proper forest management. This has signaled a common recognition that government, not the market, must make sure that the transactions between people and the earth are somewhat in balance, and that the interests of future generations are recognized by current citizens.

However, in the United States of 1985, a whopping federal deficit, coupled with a political urge to cut individual income taxes, caused the Reagan administration to propose elimination of all tax incentives favoring reforestation (and soil conservation) in the name of "tax reform." Congress did not accept those damaging changes, but the fact that it was proposed and energetically promoted by the president gave resource policy analysts pause for thought.

What this indicated was that the fate of the natural resources in the United States—and with them, the fate of future citizens—could be left entirely to the outcomes driven by market economics. For all the virtues of the market in providing a low-cost way of mediating transactions between individuals, no one has seriously proposed that the market works well for transactions between the present and the future, or for transactions between people and the environment. What President Reagan seemed to be saying, instead, was that neither of those types of transactions are much cause for concern.

Those issues, however, are critical to future economic strength and basic to national security. Forcing them to be intensely debated within the national political context—by politicians of all political persuasions—would be both timely and helpful. Whether these are "unnecessary federal spending" or "essential investments in our future" is not clearly agreed upon in the United States, and that agreement needs to be reached.

Government has a role in assuring that a balanced investment in natural resources replaces today's widespread disinvestment. It is the only institution that can create the climate in which this will be done. The 1985 Farm Bill, which removed access to federal program subsidies from farmers who convert highly erodible grass and forest lands or wetlands to crops, was a much-needed step in the right direction. The next step, taken in the 1986 Tax Reform Act, was to remove tax incentives for land abuse. Both of these steps involved no cost at all to the nation's treasury.

Guiding New Technology

Industrial and governmental scientists are close to historic breakthroughs that could result in entirely new varieties and technical methods of producing many crops. If these new technologies prove to be capable of allowing us to "engineer" the type of characteristics that emerge from the laboratory, it will be important that those who do the "engineering" are mindful of whose interests must be served by their products.

As pointed out earlier, new technologies, to be successful, must be profitable to producers as well as suppliers. A new variety that gains its improved yields through additional usage of higher-priced oil-based fertilizers and chemicals would seem to run counter to that need. Short-term fluctuations aside, the long-term prospect for oil is for scarcer supplies and higher prices. Can agricultural chemicals be more cheaply formulated out of coal, or biomass, or sea water? I must admit to technical ignorance on that score, but if there is a chance of so doing, agribusiness had better be leading the search if it intends to stay competitive.

Can varieties be designed that rely less on high inputs, that are more resilient to environmental fluctuations, and that are easily integrated into the complex management systems that seem to be emerging from the current trends in conservation tillage? Or must they be high-strung, sensitive "thoroughbreds" that need to be grown in pampered, almost sterile conditions? If the former is possible, that should be our goal. If the latter is necessary, someone needs to make sure that the old seed stocks are kept on hand.

PROFITS, NOT YIELDS, ARE THE KEY

There is considerable evidence that many of the production technologies in use today were designed with very little thought for resource conservation. Maximum yield has been the main goal—often, apparently, the only goal. As I have pointed out, these technologies have produced huge harvests but small profits. The nation would be better served if the technologies that emerge to anchor the post-Oil Age focused less on total output and more on profitable production, and more on resource protection and maintenance than on resource exploitation.

BIBLIOGRAPHY

Bauder, James W. 1984. "Projecting the Impact of Conservation Tillage." *Fertilizer Progress*, March-April 1984, p. 15.

Block, John R. 1984 "Keynote Address." In *Conservation Tillage—Strategies for the Future: Conference Proceedings*, Hal D. Heimstra and James W. Bauder, eds. Fort Wayne, Ind.: Conservation Tillage Information Center, pp. 2–8.

Clark, Edwin H. II, Jennifer A. Haverkamp, and William Chapman. 1985. *Eroding Soils: The Off-Farm Impact*. Washington, D.C.: The Conservation Foundation, p. 112.

Cook, Kenneth A. and Susan E. Sechler. 1985. "Agricultural Policy: Paying for our Past Mistakes." *Issues in Science and Technology* 2, no. 1 (Fall 1985): 97–110.

Doyle, Jack. 1985. "Biotechnology Research and Agricultural Stability." *Issues in Science and Technology* 2, no. 1 (Fall 1985): 111–124.

Foell, Richard H. 1984. "What Conservation Tillage Means to Agri-Business." In *Conservation Tillage—Strategies for the Future: Conference Proceedings*, Hal D. Heimstra and James W. Bauder, eds. Fort Wayne, Ind.: Conservation Tillage Information Center, pp. 79–80.

Gever, John, Robert Kaufmann, David Skole, and Charles Vorosmarty. 1986. *Beyond Oil: The Threat to Food and Fuel in the Coming Decades*. Cambridge, Mass.: Ballinger.

Hubbert, M. King. 1956. "Nuclear Energy and the Fossil Fuels." *Drilling and Production Practice*. Washington, D.C.: American Petroleum Institute.

Langdale, George W. and William Schrader. 1982. "Soil Erosion Effects on Soil Productivity of Cultivated Cropland." In *Determinants of Soil Loss Tolerance*, ASA Special Pub. No. 45. Madison, Wis.: American Society of Agronomy.

Larson, William E., Frank J. Pierce, and Robert H. Dowdy. 1983. "The Threat of Soil Erosion to Long-Term Crop Production." *Science* 219: 458–465.

Leman, Christopher K. and Robert L. Paarlberg. 1985 pp. 126, 138. "The Continued Political Power of Agricultural Interests." In R. J. Hildreth, Kathryn Layton, Kenneth Clayton and Carol O'Connor, eds. *Agriculture and Rural Areas Approaching the 21st Century: Challenges for Agricultural Economics*. Ames: Iowa State University Press.

Maraniss, David. 1986. "For West Texans, It's Merely Boom and Bust, as Usual." *Washington Post*, February 12, 1986, p. 1.

Nothdurft, William E. 1984. *Renewing America: Natural Resource Assets and State Economic Development*. Washington, D.C.: Council of State Planning Agencies.

Pavelis, George A. 1983. "Conservation Capital in the United States, 1935–1980." *Journal of Soil and Water Conservation* 38 (November-December 1983): 455–458.

Sampson, R. Neil. 1981. *Farmland or Wasteland: A Time to Choose*. Emmaus, Pa.: Rodale Press.

U.S. Department of Agriculture. 1980. *1980 Handbook of Agricultural Charts*. Agriculture Handbook No. 574. Washington, D.C.: U.S. Government Printing Office.

———. 1982. Soil Conservation Service. *Basic Statistics: 1977 National Resources Inventory*. Statistical Bulletin Number 686. Washington, D. C.: U.S. Department of Agriculture.

———. 1983. *1983 Handbook of Agricultural Charts*, Agriculture Handbook No. 619, Washington, D.C.: U.S. Government Printing Office.

———. 1985. *Annual RCA Progress Report: National Program for Soil and Water Conservation*. Washington, D. C.: U.S. Department of Agriculture.

———. 1987a. *1987 Fact Book of Agriculture*. Miscellaneous Publication Number 1063. Washington, D.C.: U.S. Government Printing Office.

———. 1987b. *The Second RCA Appraisal: Analysis of Condition and Trends*. Review draft. Washington, D.C.: U.S. Department of Agriculture.

U.S. Environmental Protection Agency. 1984. *Report to Congress: Nonpoint Source Pollution in the U.S.* Washington, D.C.: EPA.

Wessel, James. 1983. *Trading the Future: Farm Exports and the Concentration of Economic Power in our Food System.* San Francisco: Institute for Food and Development Policy.

Wetherbee, Robert. 1984. "What Conservation Tillage Means to the Farmer." In *Conservation Tillage—Strategies for the Future: Conference Proceedings,* Hal D. Heimstra and James W. Bauder, eds. Fort Wayne, Ind.: Conservation Tillage Information Center, pp. 77–78.

Yergin, Daniel. 1982. "Pangloss on the Energy Future: Wishful Thinking." *New York Times,* November 9, 1982, Opinion and Editorial page.

6

Agricultural Land: The Values at Stake

Pierre Crosson

ABSTRACT

Agricultural land is the source of several values: output of food and fiber, space for growing urban populations, plant and animal habitat, visual amenities, and a set of "Jeffersonian" values associated with rural life. Sediment and chemicals in runoff from agricultural land may impair recreational, ecological, and other values of clean water. The main long-term threats to this set of values are those resulting from sediment and chemicals in runoff and from loss of habitat and visual amenities. Conversion of agricultural land to urban uses and soil erosion are not long-term threats to production values; and it is not clear that management of agricultural land has imposed, or is likely to impose, significant losses of "Jeffersonian" values.

Key Words: agricultural land, values, intergenerational equity, land conversion, soil erosion, productivity, off-farm damage

INTRODUCTION

The way we manage agricultural land has important consequences for a diversity of social values we hold important. The land is a key component of the production process by which we meet demands for food and fiber. It also provides room to accommodate growing urban populations and economic activity. The open space provided by agricultural land is a source of visual amenity values for rural people and also for urban inhabitants seeking a visual alternative to crowded urban landscapes. The land provides habitat for wild plant and animal life of economic, scientific, and aesthetic value. Moreover, land management practices may pose a threat to important economic and environmental values off the farm if they result in significant erosion and runoff of chemicals. Finally, in the Jeffersonian vision of America, agricultural land is seen as a key to the preservation of important intangible values: personal independence, the democratic process, and vibrant rural communities as an antidote to the perceived spiritual corruption associated with urban life.

These diverse values have both intra- and intergenerational dimensions. How we manage the land today has important implications for values received by members of our generation, but it has implications as well for values that will be important to the next and subsequent generations. This intergenerational dimension always has been deemed important by conservationists and anyone else genuinely interested in the land as a source of social value. No serious discussion of issues in management of the land can leave this dimension out.

Issues arise because different patterns of land management have different impacts on the things we value. No single pattern will give us as much as we would like of all the values. Depending on the pattern we choose, we can have more of some values—but always at the cost of giving up a part of others. If we want a pattern that gives us more and lower-cost food and fiber, we must expect less of something else— for example, diminished water quality because of more erosion, or habitat loss from land clearing, or the spread of monocultural cropping systems. If we want to enhance visual amenity values by slowing the conversion of agricultural land to urban uses, we must expect to pay more for urban housing and business space.

The problem of choosing among alternative patterns of managing the land is the problem of establishing trade-offs among the values at stake. Somehow we must weight the values if we are to decide how much of one we are willing to give up to get more of another. The weighting of values raises large questions of social and economic choice that I do not address here. Rather, I deal with some of the principal issues concerning agricultural land that arise when those questions of choice are addressed.

These issues have to do with the factual consequences of land management practices and interpretation of the consequences. I address three sets of issues. One concerns the amount of agricultural land we are losing to conversion and its significance for things we value. The second set concerns the costs of soil erosion in lost productivity and off-farm damage, and the importance of these costs. Finally, I discuss the relationship between land management and intangible "Jeffersonian" values, which I call here values of rural life and community.

CONVERSION OF AGRICULTURAL LAND

For the last decade or so, the conversion of agricultural land to urban and transportation uses has excited much interest among those of us concerned about land management and its consequences. The view is widely held that present and prospective rates of conversion pose a threat to the nation's long-term capacity to produce food and fiber and to other social values. All states and many localities now have taken steps to slow the rate of conversion, and the 1985 Farm Bill obliged the federal government to take heed of the effects of its programs on conversion.

Rates of Conversion

Concern about conversion was heightened in the 1970s by Soil Conservation Service (SCS) surveys indicating that the rate of conversion after 1967 had almost doubled compared to the previous decade. The concern was expressed most prominently in the *National Agricultural Lands Study*, or NALS (USDA and Council on Environmental Quality, 1981). Drawing on the SCS surveys, NALS concluded that, between 1967 and 1975, some 2.1 million acres of agricultural land were converted annually to urban and transportation uses, with another 800,000 acres inundated by water. Of the 2.9 million acres converted each year, 675,000 were said to be cropland and another 200,000 were potential cropland. The annual rate of conversion was about 80 percent higher than in 1957–67.

NALS figures were sharply criticized as being too high (Fischel, 1982; Simon, 1982), and the 1982 National Resources Inventory (NRI) taken by the SCS (USDA, 1984) agreed with the critics. The NRI showed that the total urbanized area in the country in 1982 was 46.7 million acres, 18 million acres less than in the survey used by NALS. Since all other evidence indicated continuing conversions of agricultural land between the two surveys, the apparent decline is an obvious error, and the SCS acknowledges that the earlier figure was too high.

Other research indicates that in the 1970s about 1 million acres of agricultural land were converted annually to urban and transportation uses, not the 2.1 million used by the NALS (Frey, 1983). Moreover, only about 400,000 of those converted acres were cropland, not 675,000 (Dunford, 1983). Despite the continuing conversion, the total amount of cropland in the early 1980s was about the same as in the late 1960s, the cropland converted being replaced by land formerly in pasture, range, and forest.

The conversion of cropland and other agricultural land to nonagricultural uses will continue but probably at a slower rate than in the

1970s (Brown and Beale, 1981). Population is growing more slowly, and the interstate highway system—a demander of agricultural land in part of the 1970s—now is substantially complete. Some additional agricultural land will be used for strip mining of coal and siting of power plants, but the amount promises to be small—less than 2 million acres between the late 1970s and 2000 (Brewer and Boxley, 1982).

There is good reason to believe, therefore, that future conversions of cropland to nonagricultural uses will be less than the roughly 400,000 acres converted annually in the 1970s. In addition to actual conversion, urban encroachment may reduce the productivity of some cropland in or contiguous to urban areas. This effect—referred to in the agricultural land retention literature as the "impermanence syndrome"—may occur because of restrictions put on farm operations—for example, prohibiting the spraying of pesticides or early morning use of farm machinery, or because the farmer is simply awaiting an opportunity to sell to a developer and begins to take his nonland capital out of the farm, or for other reasons. NALS provides no estimates of the amount of land affected by the impermanence syndrome, and I am not aware of reliable estimates made by others.

Significance of Conversion

Even allowing for the impermanence syndrome, the prospective additional demand for cropland for nonagricultural uses seems small— less than 400,000 acres per year, plus the syndrome element—against a present and potential cropland supply of 573 million acres (USDA, 1984). These numbers imply that prospective annual conversions will not be more than 0.1 percent of the cropland base and that cumulative conversions over the next 25 years would be only 2.0 to 2.5 percent of the base.

Potential cropland—some 153 million acres according to the 1982 NRI (USDA, 1984)—is land now in forest, pasture, and range. Conversion of that land to crops or nonagricultural uses would reduce the amount available for forest or animal production. Potential cropland was about 16 percent of nonfederal land in forest, range, and pasture in 1982. However, when federal land devoted to forest and animal production is included, potential cropland falls to less than 13 percent of the land devoted to those purposes. Even if all the potential cropland were converted to crops or nonagricultural uses over the next 25 years or so—which is quite unlikely—a very modest increase in the productivity of forest and grazed land would offset the reduction in supply.

In short, the conversion of agricultural land to nonagricultural uses does not appear to be a serious threat to the nation's capacity to produce food and fiber at reasonable costs in the foreseeable future. The important economic values represented by capacity will not likely be put in jeopardy by conversion.

The impact of conversion on amenity values of open space and on values of plant and animal habitat may be less benign. A major problem in addressing this issue is that amenity values are not priced, nor are some components of habitat value. Consequently, we have no measures of the total value at stake or how much may be lost by conversion. There is reason to believe, however, that the loss is socially excessive. Neither amenity values nor unpriced habitat values are reflected in the prices of agricultural land. Consequently, prices are lower than they otherwise would be, weakening farmers' incentives to keep the land in agriculture rather than sell it to a developer.

The problem with amenity values arises because farmers have no way of charging for them. They are freely available to anyone driving or walking down a public country road or highway. Being free, amenity values are worthless to the farmer as landowner, although their value to those who enjoy them is quite real. The demand for these values is likely to grow as our society increases in population and affluence. With more income and leisure, more people will seek the pleasures of a drive or hike through open or undeveloped country.

The problem with habitat values is not quite the same because some of these values are reflected in the prices of agricultural land. The clearest case of this is habitat for game animals. People are willing to pay for access to land where they can hunt. The price for the right of access is a measure of the marginal social value of the habitat and figures in the price of the land. Consequently, when owners of agricultural land are thinking about selling to a developer, they will automatically take account of this aspect of the land's habitat value just as they do of its value for producing food and fiber.

However, the land may also produce unpriced habitat values. For example, many of today's most valuable medicinal drugs are based on plant species that once had no economic value. There is every reason to expect this experience to be repeated with other species. But because their value is only potential, dependent upon currently unforeseen advances in science and technology, these species convey no present value to the habitat where they are found. Consequently, this potential habitat value will carry no weight in farmers' decisions about selling land for development.

Thus there is substantial ground in principle for believing that the rate of agricultural land conversion is excessive because it fails to reflect the social value of open space amenities and of unpriced habitat. Whether the loss of value is practically significant, however, is quite unclear. According to the 1982 NRI, 96 percent of the surface of the United States is open space—only 4 percent being devoted to urban and built-up uses, rural transportation, and small lakes and ponds.

Future rates of urbanization will not change these percentages very much. To be sure, much of the country's open space is distant from main population centers. Still, except for the New York metropolitan area and a few other large, densely populated centers, improvements in the road system in and around urban areas have put most urban people within a 15- to 30-minute drive of open farming country. Indeed, I will hazard the guess that because of these developments people in even the largest centers have suffered little loss of access to open space in the last 20 or 30 years despite conversions of agricultural land. This says nothing about the total loss of amenity value because of conversion, only that the conversion of the last several decades probably did not increase the loss very much.

Given the potential value of unpriced habitat, the amount of loss attributable to agricultural land conversion depends on two conditions: (1) the quantity of loss of potentially valuable plant and animal species and (2) the extent to which species not threatened by conversion—or anything else—can substitute for those under threat. If the threatened species are completely extinguished and there are no substitutes for them, the loss of value is a maximum. If the species are extinguished but there are perfect substitutes for them in both quantity and quality, then the loss of value is zero. Variations in loss between zero and the maximum will depend upon variations in the two limiting conditions.

The threat posed by conversion of agricultural land to unpriced habitat values obviously raises empirical questions involving the biological and ecological sciences as well as economics. I have no answers to these questions, nor as far as I know does anyone else. Interdisciplinary research is badly needed in this area if we are to get a reasonably clear reading on what agricultural land conversion is costing us—or may cost us in the future—in lost values of unpriced habitat.

SOIL EROSION

Concern about soil erosion in the United States, from the time of Hugh Hammond Bennett in the 1930s until very recently, always was focused on loss of soil productivity as the principal threat. It was widely recognized that the threat was not primarily to productivity this year or the next. It was seen instead as a threat to the interests of future generations in being able to meet demands for food and fiber at reasonable costs.

This concern about the long-term productivity effects of erosion motivated establishment of the Soil Conservation Service in 1935 and served to justify the expenditure since then of some $60 billion (in 1980s prices) on programs related in one way or another (some quite loosely) to soil conservation.

The Lack of Information

One of the curious aspects of this experience was that at no time, from Bennett's day until the 1977 National Resources Inventory (USDA, 1980), did anyone know how much erosion was actually occurring. Nor did we have a clue as to how much it was costing us as a nation in lost production values. Conservation inventories were taken in the 1930s and repeated in 1958 and 1967. They provided useful information about the erosion condition of the land, classifying soils as uneroded or slightly eroded, moderately eroded, and severely eroded. But they included no data on the annual amounts of erosion, no doubt because measurement techniques were not sufficiently developed. The universal soil loss equation had not yet been invented.

How was it possible that over a 40-year period we could spend tens of billions of dollars to deal with a problem we knew almost nothing about? The answer lies deep in the murky processes by which, as a nation, we assign priorities among the issues we face—or think we face—and I can only skim the surface.

Rationale for Soil Conservation Spending

Four points strike me as interesting. One is that, from the beginning, and particularly in the early years, expenditures for soil conservation were intended at least as much to improve farm income as to protect the soil. If one's objective in spending money is not soil conservation then one does not need to know anything about erosion control to justify the spending. That the money came in a box marked "soil conservation" was only a minor inconvenience.

Another point is that, although scientifically valid evidence about erosion and its national productivity consequences was missing, there was much anecdotal evidence that erosion was high; and early experimental evidence was accumulating that its productivity effects were serious. Bennett used vivid language to describe the effects of erosion in the southern Piedmont, Appalachia, the southern plains, and the Corn Belt. Expressions such as "almost complete devastation," "tremendously impoverished," "suffering severely," and "virtually destroyed" flowed from his pen and his speeches around the country to describe the effects of erosion on the land in these regions (Bennett and Chapline, 1928; Bennett, 1931). Early experiment station research on erosion was beginning to show that soil productivity was in fact reduced, on some soils substantially, when the topsoil was stripped away. Thus, if one did not insist on carefully marshalled scientific evidence, one could make a case that erosion was indeed "a national menace," as Bennett called it.

A third point is the deep personal commitment of Bennett to soil conservation, and the personal force and political skill he brought to pursuit of that commitment. Combined with his solid and well-earned reputation as a soil scientist, these qualities made Bennett a formidable advocate for soil conservation within the executive branch of the federal government, before the Congress, and around the country which he crossed and recrossed to carry his message with all the fervor of an itinerant evangelist.

But—and this is the fourth point—Bennett, despite his skill and strength of personality, could not have mobilized the political support needed to launch the soil conservation movement had he not been able to tap a deeply held belief of the American people that, in managing the land, we have a moral obligation to protect the interests of future generations. It is this sense of intergenerational obligation that has sustained the soil conservation movement since the time of Bennett and the other pioneers of soil conservation, despite the absence of hard scientific evidence about erosion and its national productivity consequences.

The Erosion-Productivity Relationship

Now, within the last few years, we have begun to accumulate this evidence. Two events have made it possible. One was the collection, for the first time, of survey data showing how much erosion is occurring annually. The 1977 NRI (USDA, 1980) was an innovative undertaking by the SCS, and it was followed by the even more useful 1982 NRI (USDA, 1984).

The second event was the development of models that use the NRI data to show the long-term effects of erosion on productivity of the soil. The first of these models, called the Yield-Soil Loss Simulator (Y-SLS), was built by Paul Dyke and Linda Hagen, USDA economists, for use in the 1980 Resource Conservation Assessment (1980 RCA) done by the USDA (1981). Other models were developed subsequently by William Larson and colleagues at the University of Minnesota (Pierce et al., 1984), by Crosson at Resources for the Future (RfF) (Crosson and Stout, 1983), and by Jimmy Williams, Paul Dyke, John Putman, and their colleagues at the USDA's facility in Temple, Texas. This last model, called the Erosion Productivity Impact Calculator (EPIC), is a successor to the Y-SLS and played a central role in the USDA's 1985 Resource Conservation Assessment (USDA, 1987).

Although these four models are based on quite different approaches to the measurement of erosion-productivity relationships, they all point to the same conclusion: erosion-induced losses of productivity in the United States have been and will continue to be small. The RfF model showed that, in the Corn Belt, the annual growth of corn and soybean yields between 1950 and 1980 was about 5 percent less than it would have been had erosion had no effect on yields. Wheat yields were not affected by erosion between 1950 and 1980.

The Y-SLS, Minnesota, and EPIC models asked the question: "If present rates of erosion continue for 50 to 100 years, how much lower will yields be at the end of the period?" The Y-SLS found an 8 percent reduction at the end of 50 years, and the Minnesota and EPIC models found reductions of 3 to 5 percent after 100 years. All three models are consistent with continuing net increases in yields because of technology. In the 1985 RCA, yields are projected to increase substantially because the positive effect of technological advance is expected to far outweigh the negative effect of erosion, as measured by EPIC.

Cost of Erosion-Induced Productivity Loss

These estimates of erosion-induced losses of productivity are all stated in bushels per acre. But to judge the social value of the losses, we need to price the bushels and estimate the number of acres on which losses will occur. Moreover, because the losses are projected into the future, we need an interest rate with which to discount the losses to compute their present value.

Elsewhere (Crosson, 1988) I have estimated the total value of erosion-induced losses of crop production over the next 100 years. The annualized value of the loss is $405 million to $811 million in prices of the early 1980s. Assuming a 4 percent real rate of interest (the rate used by the USDA in calculations of this sort), the present value of the projected 100-year loss is $10.1 billion to $20.2 billion.

However, this estimate leaves out some important additional erosion costs. It does not include the costs of the extra fertilizer farmers will put on to compensate for erosion-induced soil nutrient losses or of the extra tractor fuel they will use because of erosion-induced losses of soil tilth. Nor does it include the costs of measures farmers take to hold erosion in check. Taking these additional costs into account, I estimate the total national annualized costs of erosion effects on productivity and of erosion control measures at between $2.0 billion and $2.7 billion. One half to two-thirds of this is costs of erosion control. The other half is costs of yield loss and of compensatory fertilizer and fuel.

These are estimates of the annualized loss of crop production values that continuation of present rates of erosion will impose on us over the next 100 years. Is the loss much or little? In particular, is the amount of the loss consistent with our obligation not to impose higher costs on future generations?

Based on USDA data, I conservatively estimate total average crop production costs at $55 billion annually over the five years 1979–83. The estimated costs of erosion are about 3.5–5.0 percent of this. This suggests that if we concentrate our attention only on keeping erosion costs in check, we will fail to meet our responsibilities to the future. Future costs will be dominated by the growth of domestic and foreign demand, by the prices of production inputs, and by the impact of technological change. If demand and input prices grow at 1970s rates and technology fails to keep pace, production costs will rise even if we succeed in reducing erosion costs to zero.

The commitment to intergenerational equity thus would be violated despite our best effort at erosion control. On the other hand, if demand growth, input prices, and technology behave as they did in the 1950s and 1960s, total production costs will decrease even if erosion costs were to double.

In short, prospective erosion costs are so small relative to other cost components that, if we concentrate solely—or even mainly—on controlling erosion costs, we likely will fall short in meeting our obligations to future generations. The best way to assure that we meet that obligation is to invest in research on technologies based on relatively low-cost inputs that permit farmers to stay ahead of rising demand.

OFF-FARM DAMAGE

A major difficulty with off-farm damages of erosion is that the farmers who generate the damaging sediment do not bear the cost of the damages. As a consequence, they have no incentive to control erosion to reduce the costs. If the social values threatened by off-farm erosion damages are to be adequately protected, some measure of public intervention to reduce the damages will be required.

Soil conservationists have always recognized that eroded soil may do damage when it leaves the farm, and that at some times and places the damage may be serious. But the principal concern always was with long-term effects of erosion on soil productivity, and soil conservation policy reflected this.

There now are signs at the USDA that this is beginning to change. There is a small but perceptible movement toward giving off-farm erosion damage—including water quality and aquatic habitat impacts—relatively more attention and soil productivity loss relatively less.

I do not know all the reasons for this shift, but I believe two related lines of research have played an important role. One is that just described showing that productivity losses from erosion are small. The other is work done by Edwin Clark and others at The Conservation Foundation in estimating the costs of off-farm erosion damage (Clark, Haverkamp, and Chapman 1985). Clark estimates annual off-farm costs at $3.4–$13.0 billion (1980 prices), with a "best guess" estimate of $6.1 billion. By comparison, the productivity costs of erosion—excluding control costs because Clark's estimates exclude these—are estimated at $550–600 million annually, an order of magnitude less than Clark's "best guess" estimate of off-farm costs. Clark recognized that his estimates are subject to substantial error, which is why the spread between his higher and lower numbers is so wide. But even if the lower estimate is closer to the truth, off-farm costs would be five to six times greater than the comparable costs of productivity loss.

It seems fair to conclude that current land management practices impose much higher losses of social value through off-farm erosion damage than through productivity loss. It makes sense, therefore, for the USDA to give relatively higher priority to measures for reducing off-farm damage and for the soil conservation community to support this shift.

However, we ought to recognize that reducing off-farm damage is likely to prove a far more intractable problem than reducing productivity loss. Three characteristics of off-farm damages strike me as particularly troublesome. One is the tendency of streams to carry a full capacity load of suspended sediment. If through erosion control on the land we succeed in reducing deliveries of soil to streams, many of the streams will begin to scour soil from stream banks and beds, the amounts depending on soil characteristics and the amount of excess stream carrying capacity. Consequently, success in reducing erosion on the land will not necessarily reduce the amount of damaging sediment delivered downstream. The increase in stream scour may cause additional damage—for example, by eroding soil supporting bridge abutments. These kinds of problems are not in my area of expertise, but as I read the literature and talk with people who are experts, I get the strong impression that dealing with compensating streambank scour may present major, and poorly understood, technical obstacles to development of cost-effective policies for reducing off-farm erosion damage.

A second problem is the difficulty of linking places suffering sediment damage with the places on the landscape supplying the sediment and related nonpoint-source pollutants. The movement of sediment through a watershed is a halting, complex process that may take years, decades, or even centuries. Given the initial erosion, the principal determinants of the rate and amount of soil moved are the periodicity and intensity of rainfall; size, topography, and drainage density of the watershed; kinds of soil; patterns of land use; and the volume and velocity of water available to transport sediment. The relationships among these factors evidently are not sufficiently well understood to establish reliable time and space linkages between damaging sediment and its place of origin.

This presents two problems for policy, quite apart from that of stream-bank scour: (1) we cannot be sure just when measures to control erosion in the watershed will begin to pay off in reduced sediment damage downstream, and (2) we cannot be sure just where in the watershed we should target erosion control to get the most cost-effective reduction in downstream damage.

By contrast, our ability to measure erosion and its effects on soil productivity is much stronger. Consequently we can target erosion control to reduce productivity loss much more reliably than we can target to reduce off-farm damage. Unfortunately, productivity loss is not the main problem.

The first two difficulties in dealing with off-farm erosion damages arise primarily from poor understanding of technical problems. The third is rooted in social, political, and ethical problems. Suppose that somehow the first two sets of problems have been solved so we can identify the farmers whose fields deliver damaging sediment and related pollutants downstream, and we can reliably predict that if we reduce erosion from those fields we will get corresponding reductions in downstream damages. How do we get the necessary reductions in erosion?

Traditionally, and at present, we rely on education, persuasion, and economic incentives to induce farmers to adopt erosion control measures voluntarily. These may or may not be effective, depending on how the farmer sizes up his situation, particularly with respect to economics. Of course as a society we could always induce farmers to adopt however much erosion control we want if we were willing to pay enough for it. But we never have been willing to pay that much, and in the current political climate of budget tightness we certainly are not.

Even if the money were there, the question must be asked. "Should we pay farmers to reduce off-farm erosion damage?" In principle, this kind of damage is no different from that caused by industrial wastes dumped in water or emitted to the air. We do not hesitate to regulate industrial polluters, using the police power of the state against those who fail to abide by the regulations. Why should we treat agricultural polluters any differently?

I see no reason in principle why we should. As a practical matter, however, there are some formidable difficulties facing a regulatory approach to control of off-farm damage. One flows from the technical problems in assigning responsibility for damage. If we cannot be sure where the damaging sediment is coming from, we cannot be sure who to regulate. Farmers subject to proposed regulation often will find it easy to demonstrate that the case against them has not been made. Attempts to enforce regulations in such cases not only will face political and legal resistance, but also will raise genuine issues of equity and justice. The police power of the state is a fearsome thing. No one can want to see it unleashed except where the public interest is clearly under threat and those posing the threat are clearly identified.

Even where the farmers posing the threat are known, a regulatory approach will be difficult because it runs against the much-touted tradition of "voluntarism" in erosion control. The issue here also is one of how to secure equity, but it is equity for taxpayers and downstream users of sediment-polluted waters—not farmers—that is at stake. A regulatory approach can be defended as the best way to secure equity in these circumstances, but farmers will use the political process to fight for voluntarism, and they may be successful. They have been so far. In any case, whatever combination of voluntarism and regulation we adopt, adequately protecting the social values threatened by off-farm erosion damage may prove to be very expensive.

INTANGIBLE VALUES

There is a widely held view among people concerned about the management of agricultural land that the land is a source of important intangible values. I consider two: rural life and community.

Values of Rural Life

The values I have in mind stem from the Jeffersonian tradition. In this tradition, farming promotes independence, which has value in itself but which also is vitally important to the maintenance of democratic institutions. In this perspective, farmland—when widely held among the population—provides people the means to sustain themselves economically and gives them an important stake in preservation of private property. Together these two conditions establish the basis for resistance to the imposition of governmental tyranny.

This view of the role of farming in society has been undermined by processes of socioeconomic change over the last two centuries. Under modern conditions, farmers are not noticeably more independent of economic and political forces beyond the farmgate than factory workers are of those outside the factory. Increasing interdependence is an integral part of the process of economic development. If farmers have lost Jeffersonian independence, it is because they were deeply involved in this process. The way we manage agricultural land had nothing to do with it.

The loss of independence in the Jeffersonian sense has been compensated, I believe, by a gain of independence in another sense. Independence without opportunity is meaningless, and there can be little question that farmers today have more opportunity than they did in Jefferson's time, or than they did even three or four decades ago. Data collected by the USDA (1983) indicate that, after adjustment for inflation, the income of farmers has increased substantially since the 1930s.

Indeed, it increased more than the income of the nonfarm population. This increase in income provided farmers the opportunity to expand farm operations and, perhaps most important, to acquire more education—the key to wider opportunity in all of life's activities. Moreover, the transformation of the economy from rural to urban created new off-farm job opportunities for farmers, both for those who chose to leave farming as well as for many of those who stayed behind.

As for the values of independence, there is no reason to believe that democratic values have been weakened by changes in the ways in which we manage the land. In my judgment—and I think this is widely shared—American society today is significantly more democratic than it was three or four decades ago, let alone by comparison with Jefferson's day. Blacks, Hispanics, Orientals, Jews, and Catholics have found steadily increasing access to the country's economic, social, political, and cultural life. However much remains to be done, there can be little doubt that much already has been achieved.

Values of Community

People generally put great value on feeling part of a community, and people living in rural areas are no different from others in this respect. Changes in farming that weaken the vitality of rural communities thus are seen as a threat.

There is a significant body of research (Tweeten, 1984, and others cited by him) indicating that areas characterized by small- to medium-sized owner-operated farms support more vigorous social and economic life in rural communities than areas characterized by large farms. This is especially true if the latter are absentee owned. A system of solely small- to medium-sized farms would be higher cost than the present system because small- to medium-sized farms are not as efficient as large farms (Tweeten, 1984). With only small farms, consumers would have paid 14 percent more for food than they actually did in 1981 and 19 percent more than they would have with a solely large farm agriculture (Tweeten, 1984). The cost disadvantage of a solely medium-sized farm system is about half that of a small farm system.

These results suggest that we can strengthen the values of rural community by pushing for a small- to medium-sized farm system if we are willing to accept higher costs for food. But if we opt for such a system, we ought to recognize that we would be putting the poor at a disadvantage because the poor spend proportionately more of their income for food than do the nonpoor. Would this be too high a price to pay for achieving stronger values of community? I pretend to no answer. But the question illustrates the inescapable trade-offs we must face in seeking patterns of land management that adequately capture the variety of values·we want from the land.

BIBLIOGRAPHY

Bennett, H. 1931. "The Problem of Soil Erosion in the United States." *Annals of the Association of American Geographers* 21, no. 3: 147–170.

Bennett, H. and W. Chapline. 1928. *Soil Erosion a National Menace.* Soil Conservation Service. USDA Circular No. 33. Washington, D.C.: U.S. Government Printing Office.

Brewer, M. and R. Boxley. 1982. "The Potential Supply of Cropland." In *The Cropland Crisis: Myth or Reality,* P. Crosson, ed. Baltimore: Johns Hopkins University Press for Resources for the Future.

Brown, D. L. and C. L. Beale. 1981. "Sociodemographic Influences on Land Use in Non-Metropolitan America." In U.S. Senate, Committee on Agriculture, Nutrition and Forestry, *Agricultural Land Availability.* Washington D.C.

Clark, E. H. II, J. Haverkamp, and W. Chapman. 1985. *Eroding Soils: The Off-Farm Impacts.* Washington, D.C.: The Conservation Foundation.

Crosson, P. 1986. "Soil Conservation." *Choices,* premiere edition, the American Agricultural Economics Association, Ames, Iowa.

————. 1988. *Land in American Agriculture: The Values at Stake.* Washington, D.C.: Resources for the Future, unpublished.

Crosson, P. with A. T. Stout. 1983. *Productivity Effects of Cropland Erosion in the United States.* Washington D.C.: Resources for the Future.

Dunford, R. 1983. "An Overview of Farmland Retention Issues." Report No. 83–635 ERN, Congressional Research Service. Washington, D.C.: Library of Congress.

Fischel, W. A. 1982. "The Urbanization of Agricultural Land: A Review of the National Agricultural Lands Study." *Land Economics* 58, no. 2: 236–249.

Frey, H. T. 1983. *Expansion of Urban Area in the United States: 1960–1980.* ERS Staff Report No. AGES 830615. Washington, D.C.: U.S. Department of Agriculture.

Pierce, F. J., R. H. Dowdy, W. E. Larson, and W.A.P. Graham. 1984. "Productivity of Soils in the Corn Belt: An Assessment of the Long-Term Impacts of Erosion." *Journal of Soil and Water Conservation* 39, no. 2 (March-April): 131–136.

Simon, J. 1982. "Are We Losing Farmland?" *Public Interest* 67, no. 1: 49–62.

Tweeten, L. 1984. *Causes and Consequence of Structural Change in the Farming Industry*. Washington, D.C.: Food and Agricultural Committee of the National Planning Association.

U.S. Department of Agriculture. 1980. *Basic Statistics, 1977 National Resources Inventory*. Washington, D.C.: Soil Conservation Service.

_____. 1981. *Soil Water and Related Resources in the United States: Status, Condition and Trends 1980 RCA Appraisal Part I*. Washington, D.C.: Soil Conservation Service.

_____. 1983. *Economic Indicators of the Farm Sector: Income and Balance Sheet Statistics, 1982*. ECIFS 2–2. Washington, D.C.: Economic Research Service.

_____. 1984. *1982 National Resources Inventory*. Washington, D.C.: Soil Conservation Service.

_____. 1987. *The Second RCA Appraisal: Soil, Water and Related Resources on Nonfederal Land in the United States*. Washington, D.C.: Soil Conservation Service.

U.S. Department of Agriculture and Council on Environmental Quality. 1981. *National Agricultural Lands Study Final Report*, Washington, D.C.

7

Siting Industrial Facilities in the Western United States

Joseph B. Browder

ABSTRACT

This chapter reviews elements of the conflicts about siting of large industrial facilities, particularly energy facilities, in the western United States. It concludes that generic concerns about the need for and economics of major energy facilities have become as important as site-specific impact considerations, and that these generic concerns tend to make ambiguous what most project sponsors have traditionally seen as clear-cut guidelines for facility siting. It is suggested that currently evolving changes in economic and energy policy are creating a yet different climate for facility planning, one in which many assumptions about the goals of industry and its critics will be challenged.

Key Words: energy, energy conservation, land use, planning environment, siting, public lands, natural resources, electric power, regulation, pollution

INTRODUCTION

When industrial development requires the use of large amounts of land in areas where dominant land uses have been agricultural or recreational, conflicts are inevitable. The introduction of an airport, power plant, mine, or synthetic fuel facility into such areas will cause permanent damage to some resources and temporary damage to others, and will force many surviving resources—and human communities—

into different, more complex relationships with changed physical, cultural, and economic environments.

The process of weighing the damages and negative changes that might be caused by industrial development against a project's benefits and positive changes has always been difficult. Much of the power of local government and an increasing amount of power vested in the state and federal governments has been established to broker conflicts among private interests—and between private interests and various publics— over benefits and costs of competing land uses. Government action at all levels has led to many fairly well defined processes and standards for evaluating proposed industrial sites.

Political and economic developments of the past 15 years have greatly diminished the utility of these rules. Technical compliance with site-specific environmental standards, and the demonstration of positive local economic impacts, no longer assure a receptive response from state and federal regulators and land managers. Particularly in the West, where government agencies exercise considerable discretion about how best to use federally owned lands, the judgment of land managers and regulators has been influenced by broader considerations: the opinions of agricultural interests, environmental and consumer groups, governors, key state and federal legislators, Indian tribes, and others with policy or political concerns.

For the most part, industry has been slow to understand and accept this change. As a result, billions of dollars in planned investments have been delayed or canceled because of failure to site and plan properly, or failure to effectively advocate projects that do comply with sound environmental, economic, and social standards but are opposed for other reasons. Other projects, more responsive to changed circumstances, have moved expeditiously through the new regulatory environment.

Now, additional changes are taking place that are making the energy facility development process even more complex, but at the same time are creating new opportunities for some developers. Many regulators and much of the environmental community are as slow and reluctant to understand these new changes as was industry in responding to the changes of almost two decades ago.

SITING: EMERGENCE AS A NATIONAL ISSUE

In the 1960s and 1970s, sponsors of some controversial major developments used the resources and authority of the federal government to advance their projects, emphasizing the public purposes of and governmental interests in the proposed facilities. This emphasis reinforced efforts by environmentally motivated project opponents to transform regional conflicts into national debates, and sharpened the adversarial skills of the environmental community. The newly honed citizen-group skills were put to use, in both the national policy debates and in project-specific conflicts, when industry and government responded to the 1973 Arab oil embargo with proposals to use federal authority in behalf of the energy industry. But, with rare exceptions, federal efforts to overcome local and state interests or to weaken environmental goals in support of energy facilities produced few results, and in many cases created problems for otherwise trouble-free projects.

Increased Influence of Environmental Interests

In the late 1960s and early 1970s, three proposed developments resulting from cooperation between government and industry stimulated concerted, national opposition from organized environmental interests. Indeed, these proposals—a dam in the Grand Canyon, the world's largest airport in the Everglades, and the Trans-Alaska Pipeline—helped shape the current structure, goals, and tactics of the national environmental community in the United States. Each conflict involved, from the environmental perspective, defense of natural values within undeveloped, largely federally owned lands against proposals to site facilities that, as proposed, posed serious threats to the natural environment. Each required disparate national and local environmental interests to form coalitions, to attempt to develop new kinds of legal, technical, and economic competence, to display increased determination to educate and influence their own members, the press, and the government, and to become participants in economic development decisions that previously had been the exclusive province of business, labor, and government.

Each conflict resulted in abandonment or modification of the proposed project. Equally significant, each conflict led to policy changes with impacts felt far beyond the boundaries of the sites in question. Federal interagency disputes over the Everglades jetport helped prompt the late Senator Henry Jackson (D-Wash.) and other congressional leaders to enact the National Environmental Policy Act (NEPA).

Later, litigation over the inadequate initial environmental impact statement (EIS) for the Trans-Alaska Pipeline demonstrated that NEPA must be honestly complied with, or federally approved projects would face delay. The Grand Canyon dam conflict had a more complex result: stimulation—with initial support from the environmental leaders who stopped the dam—earlier than would otherwise have occurred of major coal-fired plants in the Southwest to supply California's then apparently insatiable appetite for electricity.

Of greatest interest, for purposes of this analysis, was the general result for siting policy: at a time when the growth of the national environmental community was encouraged by many other issues, environmentalists were forced, by the course of events, to develop a special interest and political competence in conflicts over siting. The environmental sector thus became prepared to participate actively in national siting policy just as an international crisis—the Arab oil embargo of 1973—made energy and energy facility siting issues of paramount national importance.

Industry and Government Raise the Stakes

By the time concern about the Arab oil embargo reinforced industry worries about the timely siting of energy facilities, siting questions had already begun to grow beyond specific conflicts. Although Congress's brief flirtation with national land-use planning in the early 1970s, led again by Sen. Henry Jackson, was described as environmental legislation, the proposed bills were actually designed to encourage states to preempt the ability of local governments to oppose major energy facilities. The legislation died, partly because of opposition from antiplanning interests that rejected or failed to understand utility industry siting concerns, and partly because key environmental leaders quietly but effectively opposed the legislation.

Again, a major policy consequence of that debate was the impact on some of the most active national environmental organizations: increased interest in siting as a policy issue, not just as a project-specific question centered on individual development proposals. Industry leaders seeking to further centralize the role of government in approving major facilities failed, and their attempt to do so elevated the issue on the agenda of the environmental community.

Unhappily, during a time when rational analysis of energy and energy siting needs would have served the nation well—and a time, coincidentally, when interests skeptical about claims in behalf of new energy development became influential in national policy—energy development proponents in government and industry created expectations and fears that led to even more intense conflict.

In today's climate, with industry making highly visible efforts to encourage energy conservation and displaying a post-Watt understanding (James G. Watt was President Ronald Reagan's first Secretary of the Interior. He was widely perceived in this country to be both in favor of aggressive natural resource exploitation by the private sector and in opposition to modern notions of environmental protection and government regulatory activity in the health, safety, and environment areas. He became a political liability due to the above plus some insensitive and politically inept public statements, and left the cabinet under pressure.) that concern about environmental protection cannot be ignored, it may be difficult to understand the importance of the conflicts that were so prominent from 1970 through 1976—and that flared again from 1981 through 1983.

OPEC oil price increases and the Arab oil embargo shocked the world economy and gave energy policy a more prominent place on the U.S. political agenda. Industry and government reaction to the economic and national security implications of more costly, less reliable world oil supplies produced some predictable but very unproductive consequences: among them, a national debate about energy production and facility siting that created unrealistic expectations among energy developers and stimulated even stronger opposition to some energy developments.

Development proponents projected highest-case scenarios for energy production and conversion. Early reports such as the north-central power study of the Bureau of Reclamation and later documents produced by a succession of federal energy agencies predicted the construction of hundreds of large new coal-fired and nuclear power plants, synthetic fuel plants, and oil refineries, accompanied by a massive expansion of coal, uranium, shale, and offshore oil production. Government and some industry leaders spoke glibly about the need for economic activities of considerable regional importance in many parts of the United States—for example, farming, ranching, and commercial fishing—to make way for the obviously more important energy industry. The magnitude of damage to existing values in the West was predicted to be so great that one federally commissioned study suggested that some regions might simply have to be declared "national sacrifice areas."

At the same time, energy development proponents in government and industry projected strongly negative attitudes about two issues—energy conservation and environmental protection—that enjoyed support from most of the American public. Energy production proponents reacted to energy conservation and environmental protection as if these policies were alternatives rather than conditions of, continued expansion of energy production.

The stage was thus set for an interesting period of conflict. When the Ford Foundation published a thoughtful study suggesting that energy conservation could moderate the growth of energy use without diminishing economic productivity, many oil and gas industry leaders denounced the study as subversive nonsense (Landsberg, et al. 1979). The federal government's energy policy manager (one of many to hold that unenviable post during the past several years) reflected the U.S. auto industry's belief and proclaimed that, no matter how costly gasoline might become, Americans would never become attracted to small, fuel-efficient cars and should not be encouraged to do so.

The mining and utilities industries persuaded two successive administrations, those of Nixon and Ford, to oppose federal legislation requiring the reclamation of lands strip-mined for coal, more careful economic management in the sale of federally owned coal to private mining companies, environmental protection and monitoring during production of offshore oil, and planning to protect agricultural and wildlife uses of federally owned lands when mining takes place. At the height of these debates, a leading mining industry spokesman, asked about the impact of greatly expanded coal strip mining on wildlife and agriculture in the West, said: "We never promised you a rose garden."

The important environmental legislation was passed: One bill became law after the Congress overrode a presidential veto during the Ford administration. Others attracted so much obvious congressional support that enactment took place in spite of White House opposition, and the surface mining reclamation legislation, after twice being vetoed by President Ford, became law in the first year of the Carter administration.

However, the transition from Republican to Democratic control of the White House included an ironic surprise for environmentalists: while the Republican leadership had resisted enactment or enforcement of individual energy-related environmental laws, the White House under Presidents Nixon and Ford showed little interest in bringing federal authority to bear on the siting of nonnuclear facilities.

It was the Carter administration, with strong support from key Democratic leaders in the House and Senate, that supported enactment and enforcement of laws to protect the environment, but also worked vigorously to neutralize those laws where federal environmental protection, or state and local regulations, might interfere with the siting of energy facilities. The policies of President Carter were particularly contradictory, since the numbers of coal mines, power plants, transmission corridors, and other energy projects actually licensed during the Carter administration—with no help from proposed laws supposedly needed to expedite the process—greatly exceeded the number of energy facilities permitted during the previous Nixon or Ford administrations or the subsequent Reagan administrations.

President Carter's proposed Energy Mobilization Board (EMB), lacking even the planning window-dressing of Senator Jackson's earlier land-use proposals, would have given the federal government unprecedented power and influence over local and state land use and economic development decisions.

In the end, an unusual coalition defeated the federal siting bill. Environmentalists, some industry leaders who believed that legislation was unnecessary and unworkable, and conservatives opposed to greater centralization of federal authority prevailed over those in industry who hoped to use expanded federal power to overcome local or state objections to their projects, and over federal political figures who wanted to demonstrate they were doing something, workable or not, about the energy crisis.

The Abstract and Particular Converge

For industry, the prolonged debate had a very negative consequence: many projects proposed during this period were judged not simply on their own merits, but as symbols of the larger development and policy agenda being promoted by industry. By this time, consumer and environmental critics had begun not only to analyze the specific environmental and economic consequences of individual projects, but also to challenge the basic credibility of industry's and government's judgment about the need for energy projects.

Maps showing the combined projections of industry groups and federal agencies called for so many energy facilities in the West that the Northern Plains and Rocky Mountain states, from Montana to New Mexico, appeared filled with new projects. On the Atlantic, Gulf, and Pacific coasts, the prospects of exporting U.S. coal to Europe and the Orient brought forth plans for development of new coal terminals wherever rails or barges could link the coalfields to the coastline, with total projected capacities far beyond even the most imaginative coal export scenarios. Each proposed port or plant or mine, of course, was cited by proponents as being essential to the survival of the U.S. econony.

This boosterism—with the hope of federal subsidies or federal intervention against environmental and planning standards—made it seem possible for every entrepreneur or any community to promote a nationally important energy center. Energy development took on the pork-barrel character (and the visibility) normally associated with the politically equitable distribution of federal transportation, waterways, or defense spending.

Those in the energy business who went beyond boosterism to identify real markets—and who proposed to open real mines, power or synfuel plants, transmission lines or pipelines—were forced to operate in an increasingly difficult regulatory climate. The extraordinary number of facilities called for by industry trade groups and federal energy agencies either were not believed by citizen groups, in which case the "We need this one" claims by a project sponsor were also suspect, or, for those who gave credence to the industry's plans to build hundreds of facilities, an individual project represented the first skirmish of a full-scale assault by unacceptable numbers of facilities. In either case, citizens were inspired to keep the first plants or mines out.

Looking at three proposals during the 1970s to construct large coal-fired generating plants in the Southwest in order to supply power to California, it is possible to see the development of the need issue as an element of individual debates, and to see a relationship between the importance of the need issue and the extent of conflicts over site-specific environmental problems. During the conflict over the proposed Kaiparowits project in southern Utah, opponents questioned the need for the plant, but those arguments were secondary to the more politically effective arguments about protection of the outstanding air quality in nearby national parks. The subsequent debate over the Allen-Warner Valley project in Utah and Nevada which, as was the case with Kaiparowits, was abandoned by its sponsors after a lengthy regulatory battle, was stimulated by conflicts—impacts on vistas from Bryce Canyon National Park—over the project's proposed coal supply; but ultimately it was dominated by a sophisticated argument about need for the project. Opponents turned state and federal reviews of the project into a broad debate over California energy policy.

Yet in the case of Intermountain Power Project (IPP), an even larger California-sponsored power plant being proposed in Utah at the same time as the Allen-Warner Valley project, the need question was not part of the debate, because all environmental objections to the facility were muted after federal, state, and company officials cooperated to move the project away from a site in southern Utah to a less sensitive location elsewhere in the state. Indeed, when, after all federal and state approvals had been obtained, the size of the IPP project was cut in half, the reduction took place not because of objections from the environmental groups so concerned about California energy planning, but at the insistence of a Utah investor-owned utility with a minority ownership in the project.

INDUSTRIAL FACILITY DEVELOPMENT TODAY

Because of the national debates that began 20 years ago and spawned a permanent, skeptical, and highly professional citizen capability to deal with siting issues, the business of siting industrial facilities has changed. Local interests—and even geographically remote interests linked through national (and now international) networks—influence decisions that two decades ago were made almost exclusively by industry. However, the economic and social coalitions that reinforced the power of environmental organizations in the 1970s are changing, and the economic and scientific complexity of the local and global implications of some environmental issues is straining the resources of some players in the national environmental community. At the same time, some individual companies are becoming more sophisticated in their understanding of the relationship between business opportunity and environmental-social issues. As a result, at both the policy and project-specific levels, opportunity has increased for well-operated companies to achieve their development goals.

New Rules, New and Changing Players

It is now understood by most participants that the nature of facility siting debates has changed. Proponents, regulators, and the public must weigh not only the traditional issues but also complex questions about the economy's need for the products of a proposed facility and whether, if the need exists, it might be better satisfied through alternative sites or alternative technologies. The political-regulatory climate for siting all major facilities has absorbed many components of the electric power generation siting process. Whether or not a formal part of the regulatory agenda, concerns about environmental and other trade-offs involved in industrial development—and industry's own use of broad national objectives in support of individual facilities—have made society's need for a project an element of governments' decisions to approve, reject, or modify project applications.

In the energy area the authority of government, and therefore the public, is often direct and specific with regard to not just if or where a facility should be built, but also the technologies and resources that can make up a project. For other industries, government's and the public's interest in economic need, technology, and resources may not be spelled out in the regulatory charter, but can be and are enforced through an agency's ability to delay or deny a permit for other, more official reasons.

Government's overt influence over energy industry decisions is not new. There has not been, since the inception of the organized energy industry, a genuinely market-driven decision process. National policy, federal and state economic incentives (largely expressed through tax policy), have always favored some segments of the industry more than others. Now, new rules, stimulated by state officials and environmental and consumer groups, are contributing to other changes in the way energy investment decisions are made. But the consequences are not entirely those anticipated by their authors.

The electric utility industry, because of its sanctioned-monopoly economic structure, has long been the most scrutinized and regulated sector of the energy business. The existing regulatory regime made it easier for new regulatory schemes to be imposed on the electric power industry than on other sectors. As an example, congressional efforts in the 1970s—authored by Ralph Nader, opposed by environmental interests—to establish a federally owned oil exploration corporation failed. The proposal was rejected as unnecessarily intrusive into an activity where private enterprise had always been responsible for investment decisions. Yet, although most Americans purchase their electricity from investor-owned utility companies, Congress acted with enthusiasm to change the ways in which electric power is financed, owned, produced, and distributed.

While there were many motives and multiple interests supporting the Public Utility Regulatory Policy Act of 1978 (PURPA), the merger of consumer and environmental interests that made enactment of PURPA possible resulted from one primary objective: a belief on the part of most environmental leaders that PURPA would encourage alternatives to traditional central-station electric generating plants, and thus reduce the number of sites demanded by the utility industry. This, in turn, would reduce the impact of the utility industry and its fuel suppliers on water supply, air quality, public safety, fish and wildlife habitat, and recreation areas.

The environmental strategy was fruitful. Alternative cogeneration power sources, subsidized by high consumer prices required by federal and state laws, are filling needs that otherwise would be met through expansion of utility production capacity. Late 1970s environmental responses to the siting excesses presented by industry advocates in the early 1970s are, in the 1980s, contributing to a restructuring of the U.S. electric power industry.

Technological and economic changes would have resulted in changes for the utility industry under any circumstances. But the debates of the 1970s both reinforced the economic strength of competitors to the utility industry, and made it difficult for the utilities themselves to respond to changing markets and take advantage of new technologies and resulting business opportunities.

Because the utility industry was seen by citizens as resistant to change and insensitive to the impacts of siting traditional facilities, the rules of the game were changed to give different players the edge in meeting new markets with new technologies.

Consumer and Environmental Interests: New Changes

One source of strength for critics of energy industry proposals during the 1970s was a coincidence between environmental and consumer interests. As it happened, many of the most visible and environmentally objectionable energy proposals were also extraordinarly costly—so costly and so inefficient that only federal subsidies could put them into the marketplace. Apart from the high per-unit cost of energy to be produced by the subsidized projects, it became apparent that some energy industry leaders and their advocates in government thought it necessary to keep the price of all energy high, in order to better justify the high cost of the subsidized products. From the time of former Secretary of State Henry Kissinger's management of the U.S. government's response to the Arab oil embargo through the policies advocated by the Carter administration's energy czar James Schlesinger, keeping world— and U.S.—energy prices up in order to stimulate a market for otherwise uncompetitive fuels (oil shale, coal gasification, and coal liquefaction) was considered essential.

The economic irrationality of so much of the energy industry's agenda made it easier for the industry's environmental critics to be politically credible—or at least more credible than industry advocates—in commenting on energy policy and specific projects. For most national environmental organizations, however, energy economic issues were and remain difficult to address.

Obviously, fewer synthetic fuel plants would be sited if federal subsidies were denied. But some groups wanted more environmentally benign systems to get tax subsidies, and a few proponents of solar energy have continued to be willing to support subsidies for projects considered by environmentalists to be damaging if that could translate into acceptance of subsidies for solar energy.

For more than a decade, the environmental community was able to escape any significant negative consequences from its support of high energy prices to stimulate conservation, because the energy industry itself was an even more visible advocate of even higher prices, albeit for other reasons. So the industry inevitably assumed any burden associated with public concern about cost.

But changes in energy prices have made some assumptions and some interest-group partnerships of the 1970s vulnerable to change. For several years, independent power producers were able to escape serious scrutiny of the consumer cost implications of substituting independent power for power produced by the utilities themselves. High profits to independent producers could be guaranteed by forcing utilities to purchase power from the independents, at a cost well above that of the producer, but still somewhat below what it would cost the utility to make its own power. Between the high cost of other options open to the utilities, and the relatively small percentage of independent power in a utility's system, forcing utilities to buy power from the independents had little impact on utility customers.

Now, in some jurisdictions, high-priced electricity forced onto the system by independent producers has become the largest source of new power for utilities. In addition to concerns about costs, regulators are reviewing the stability implications of dependence on large amounts of independently produced power. While many independent projects are sound and stable, the economic attractiveness of others rests on tax benefits and price subsidies subject to change, with worrisome implications for the commitment of investors to maintain reliability of performance.

A lengthy period of low oil prices, the end of subsidies for synthetic fuels, and deficit-induced pressure on government revenues and spending have changed the policy climate for energy, environmental, and economic issues. Changing economics does not suggest that long-standing support from consumers and the general public for strong and costly environmental standards is eroding. Political and industry leaders who have from time to time attempted to invoke the interest of the consumer in order to relax environmental standards have not been found credible. Public support for environmental protection continues to be strong.

What does appear to be happening is a more widespread acceptance that the economic consequences of energy and natural resource policies—including those advocated by the environmental community—must be better understood. Where the amount of environmental protection demanded by the public can be achieved with less economic disruption, environmentalists will have trouble gaining support for more costly or more disruptive options.

The dramatic illustration of this change in the public and political attitudes is the failure of the environmental community to achieve its acid rain goals. National environmental groups supported proposals that would advance the economic interests of polluting midwestern utilities and their coal suppliers while imposing high costs on western utilities and others that have already cleaned up their facilities.

The regional economic favoritism, while offering subsidies to the utilities most responsible for producing the pollution that helps cause acid rain, would have punished those companies and regions that had already paid to prevent pollution. Instead of diminishing concern about the cost of acid rain protection, the environmentalists' strategy made the economic issue even more important, and in a negative way, to other interests, thus prolonging the political stalemate.

Similarly, in spite of overwhelming public and congressional support for strong and costly measures to clean up toxic wastes, the low level of benefits achieved by the costly Superfund program, and questions about the performance of costly asbestos removal programs, have made concern about cost-effectiveness a larger element in public and congressional assessments of environmental programs. All of this translates into opportunity for industry to be better able to introduce economic considerations into project-siting debates—so long as the economic issues center on how to best achieve environmental protection, rather than proposing economic benefits as a substitute for environmental protection.

What Is Happening Now?

It is always easier to look back and attempt to explain the past than to understand the significance of current events, but some issues are emerging as indicators of present trends.

The electric power business, for decades one of the more stable, predictable elements of our economy, is changing rapidly and will change even more in the next few years. The nature of these changes makes it essential for those who hope to understand or influence facility siting policy to recognize that traditional assumptions—even recently adopted assumptions—must be constantly reviewed and challenged. The unique insight of five years ago may be this year's conventional wisdom and next year's stubborn and counterproductive mythology.

For many years environmentalists and consumers were concerned that the utility industry was encouraged, almost required, to build new facilities, because such construction offered the most secure way for stockholders to increase the return on their investments. Now, in most jurisdictions, it is the nonutility independent investors who are assured that someone—the utilities and their consumers—must pay them a certain price for producing electric power, whether it is needed or not.

The utilities themselves operate in the opposite climate: clear signals from regulators that there is little assurance that utility investment in new facilities can be recovered from rate payers. As a result, some utilities that do face increased growth in the 1990s and beyond are looking now at nontraditional, market-oriented options, considering projects that would not be placed in a sponsor's rate base, but developed with all risks and all rewards going to the investors. Other utilities are taking a wait-and-see attitude, hoping that regulators will be put in the position of urging utilities to develop new projects.

The long-term environmental and consumer implications of these differing regulatory signals being sent to utility and independent power producers are interesting. Environmentally concerned citizens, particularly at the local level, are just now beginning to understand the difficulties of dealing with the environmental impacts of projects sponsored by independent business interests rather than by highly visible and closely regulated utilities. Many consumer and public power advocates supported the programs that are now reshaping the industry because the programs were initially seen as threatening the monopoly power of big investor-owned utilities. But the largest investor-owned utilities will probably become even larger, as they absorb the less financially healthy neighboring utilities that have been unable to survive the changes in the industry.

To add, as a final note of uncertainty, concern about the global atmospheric consequences of burning fossil fuels will lead to a renewed debate over the merits of nuclear power. Whether the nuclear and utility industries are able to deal with the issues more successfully in the next debate than they did in the last one remains to be seen. Whatever the outcome, the debate will focus even more public attention on the basic issue of injecting controversial technology into local communities.

CONCLUSIONS

Most site-specific environmental aspects of facility development are, or can be, well understood. It must be assumed that a project that would degrade a national park, violate air or water quality standards, or damage important wildlife habitat is not likely to survive the predictable opposition of environmental groups and federal, state, and local regulators. Few developers in today's market are now willing to risk time and resources on such ventures that predictably would fail to meet environmental standards.

For most projects, conflict will come not because of failure or inability to comply with legal requirements, but because of failure to understand the more ambiguous questions raised by a project's intrusion into the existing environment. Debates about individual projects will continue to be influenced by broader policy issues, particularly regarding the public's views about the need for a proposed facility. Local citizens and the environmental community do not—and should not—concede that whatever is not prohibited is always permitted.

Neither, however, should it be assumed that environmental criticisms and strategies that were valid in the 1970s are necessarily effective in responding for developments planned for the 1990s. Requirements for cleaning up the abuses that created existing pollution problems may not provide sound guidance for working now to prevent future pollution, and may even frustrate the introduction of superior technologies, fuels, and systems for controlling dangerous wastes.

In the energy area, policies that once protected consumers and the environment by stimulating more diverse approaches to power generation and use may now actually retard the reliable incorporation of the best fuels and technologies into electric power systems, the automobile industry, and the waste management business.

Perhaps most importantly it should be recognized that what can be seen as siting conflicts will, over the next several years, also be forums in which decisions are made about whether technologies that reconcile the world's environmental and economic needs are developed and whether they are developed in the United States or by enterprises from Europe and Asia. If opposition to new manufacturing, energy production, and waste treatment projects in the U.S. retards the investment of U.S. companies in newer and better systems, our economy will suffer because U.S. companies will not be leaders in the growing world markets; and the global environment will suffer because the strength and initiative of the U.S. environmental community and U.S. industry and labor will become more removed from the forums where the important decisions about global economic development and environmental protection are made.

BIBLIOGRAPHY

Berkman, Richard L. and W. Kip Viscusi. 1973. *Damming the West*. New York: Grossman Publishers.

Carter, Luther J. 1974. *The Florida Experience: Land and Water Policy in a Growth State*. Baltimore: Johns Hopkins University Press for Resources for the Future.

Cicchetti, Charles J. 1972. *Alaskan Oil: Alternative Routes and Markets*. Baltimore: Johns Hopkins University Press for Resources for the Future.

Clawson, Marion. 1983. *The Federal Lands Revisited*. Baltimore: Johns Hopkins University Press for Resources for the Future.

Clean Air Act of 1970 (42 USC §1857 et seq.).

Duerksen, Christopher J. 1983. *Environmental Regulation of Industrial Plant Siting: How to Make It Work Better*. Washington, D.C.: The Conservation Foundation.

Enthoven, A. C. and A. M. Freeman III, eds. 1972. *Pollution, Resources and the Environment*. New York: W. W. Norton.

Environmental Policy Division. 1973. *National Land Use Policy Legislation: 93rd Congress*. Washington, D.C.: U.S. Government Printing Office.

Kneese, Allen and F. Lee Brown. 1981. *The Southwest Under Stress*. Baltimore: Johns Hopkins University Press for Resources for the Future.

Kresege, David T., Thomas A. Morehouse, and George W. Rogers. 1977. *Issues in Alaska*. Seattle: University of Washington Press.

Landsberg, Hans et al. 1979. Report by a Study Group: *Energy the Next Twenty Years*, sponsored by the Ford Foundation, administered by Resources for the Future. Cambridge, Mass.: Ballinger.

Linowes, David F. et al. 1984. *Report of the Commission on Fair Market Value Policy for Federal Coal Leasing*. Washington, D.C.: U.S. Government Printing Office.

National Environmental Policy Act (42 USC §4321 et seq.).

Richardson, Elmo. 1973. *Dams, Parks and Politics: Resources Development and Preservation in the Truman Eisenhower Era*. Lexington: University of Kentucky Press.

Surface Mining Control and Reclamation Act of 1977 (30 USC §1201 et seq.).

Thompson, Dennis L., ed. 1972. *Politics, Policy and Natural Resources*. New York: The Free Press.

8

Acid Rain: The Cross-Media Aspects

John A. Thorner

ABSTRACT

The cross-media aspects of acid rain have created debate among constituencies concerned with our air, our water, and our land. The forest products industry is concerned about the interaction of all three, especially how they impact the health of the trees it depends upon for its livelihood. Some observers have claimed that acid deposition damages forest health. The forest industry, however, after much investigation, believes that legislation directed at sulfur dioxide and nitrogen oxides—the precursors to acidic deposition—would be difficult to justify based on what we now know about forest health.

Key Words: acidic deposition, acid rain, forest health, forest industry, ozone, forest stress, cross-media pollution, air pollution, National Council of the Paper Industry for Air and Stream Improvement

INTRODUCTION

In no other environmental issue is the interrelationship of air, water, and land more obvious than in the acid rain phenomenon. The cross-media aspects of acid rain have created debate among constituencies concerned with our air, our water, and our land, including their use. The forest products industry, concerned with the interaction of all three, has repeatedly examined the factors that affect forest growth, for this industry's very existence depends upon healthy forests.

Acid rain is believed to result when sulfur and nitrogen compounds are released into the air, mixed with other chemical substances, and returned to the earth as acidified rainfall far from the source of the original emissions. Studies of acid rain—or, more broadly, acidic deposition—date back at least 100 years.[1] In the mid 1970s, claims that acid rain was damaging water bodies in northeastern United States and Canada gained increasing attention. More recently, some observers have suggested that acidic deposition damages forests as well.[2]

Public concern about acid rain led Congress in 1980 to wisely call for a ten-year research effort to better understand this extraordinarily complex phenomenon.[3] Lately, it also has led to considerable pressure for quick federal or state legislative "solutions" to the so-called acid rain problem.[4] The forest products industry believes, however, that legislation directed at sulfur dioxide and nitrogen oxides—the precursors to acidic deposition—would be difficult to justify based on what we now know about forest health.

INDUSTRY CONCERN

This is not to say that the forest products industry is unconcerned about the potential threat to our forests. Any threat to forest health certainly concerns the industry. This holds whether the threat comes from insects, disease, wildfire, and wind or from the possible effects of air pollution. Companies are concerned not only about the health of 70 million acres of forest land they own themselves, but also about the hundreds of millions of acres owned by government and by private individuals. That is why, collectively, companies in the forest products industry spend tens of millions of dollars annually on all kinds of programs to make forests and woodlands healthier and more productive.

Indeed, the time, money, and resources devoted by the industry to the acid rain phenomenon are extensive. But the industry believes that to assume that this phenomenon is damaging forests and to accordingly call for immediate pollution controls is a much too simplistic dismissal of a complex interaction of the very cross-media environmental factors under discussion here. Rather, the forest products industry is convinced that getting better information about what is going on in the woods is the logical first step for assuring the health of U.S. forests.

Right now, the industry has no credible evidence suggesting region-wide forest damage or decline that could be linked to acid rain or air quality problems. In each of the more limited areas where problems have been identified, scientists have suggested a number of possible causes. Climate, disease, and drought all have been implicated. Air quality may or may not be involved in some locations.[5]

NO ACID RAIN LINK

Most researchers, however, now discount any link between acid rain and forest health. Their inquiries are focused instead on other forms of pollution, especially gases such as ozone. Many of the hypotheses now being explored are new; and each one, if there truly is a forest health problem, suggests a different strategy for dealing with it.[6]

It should be pointed out that forests are subject to many different kinds of stresses—some natural such as drought and some caused by man, including accidental fire. These stresses can work singly or together to affect a forest's health. Since 1900, there have been five widespread episodes where major tree species have declined. Scientists have explained some but not all of such declines. The period between 1900 and 1925, for example, was the most prolonged and pronounced period of growth decline for ponderosa pine in the Northwest over the last 700 years.

In recent years, spruce budworm has devastated millions of acres of North American forests. In just one state, Maine, 7.5 million acres have been invaded by the insect pest since 1976.[7] In 1985 alone, about 1.8 million acres of forest were defoliated in 12 northeastern states by the gypsy moth.[8] Other pests, such as the pine beetle, pose similar threats to western and southern forests.

Air pollution can certainly be one of those stresses. We know that extremely heavy and prolonged doses of ozone have damaged forests in the San Bernardino Mountains of Southern California. Sulfur dioxide from nearby sources, such as smelters, have damaged forests near Trail, British Columbia. Our search for answers in these and other areas is complicated by the fact that very little monitoring of air pollutants is done in the forests. Rather, federal and state governments traditionally have limited their air pollution monitoring to areas in and around urban centers. We therefore do not know as much as we should about air pollution levels on remote forested lands.[9]

ISOLATED DAMAGE

We do know, however, that isolated instances of trees dying in the northeast and southeast have occurred. Camel's Hump in Vermont and Mount Mitchell in North Carolina are both places where unexplained damage to red spruce trees has been reported. These mountain-top forests are highly stressed by cold temperatures and high wind velocity, and they are often bathed in cloud moisture that can be more acidic than rain. Other possible causes for the decline have been suggested— some natural, some not. Professor Arthur Johnson of the University of Pennsylvania, for example, suggests climate may be part of the problem.

One of his theories is that an excess of nitrogen could have kept the trees growing later into the winter, thus making them more susceptible to frost damage.[10]

On Mount Mitchell, North Carolina State University scientist Robert Bruck believes that high ozone levels, more airborne nitrogen than could be absorbed by the vegetation, and heavy metals—including lead and aluminum—might all be implicated along with a possible insect infestation. "Anybody who's going around saying acid rain is killing the forest is not telling the truth," he told the *Charlotte* (N.C.) *Observer*.[11] Dr. John Barber, former executive vice-president of the Society of American Foresters, summed up the view held by professional foresters from government, academia, and the private sector. They're concerned about the effect of air pollutants deposited on forests, "but we need to know more about the pollutants and their effects before we can prescribe solutions to the problems."[12]

For decades, the industry has conducted extensive research programs—all aimed at making certain that U.S. forests are healthy and growing, and stay that way. Most of this research was aimed at attacking big, visible problems—such as disease and insects—or toward developing superior trees capable of resisting these threats. Extensive research on the effects of acidic deposition on forests, on the other hand, just began around 1980. Since then, many questions have been answered, but many more have been raised. They point to the need to consider all pollution stress factors—ozone, cloud acidity, heavy metals, and so on—before determining what kind of regulatory program, if any, is needed to help protect forest health.

RESEARCH SUPPORTED

That is why the industry is supporting vastly accelerated research—its own and massive federal programs—on the effects of air pollution on forest health. Federal funding on forest health research was more than $10 million in fiscal year 1986. The industry, along with its scientists and professional foresters, is participating in directing many of these programs. Because the industry believes that careful research is the method to follow in attacking any cross-media pollution problem, the research steps taken so far on the acid rain problem are reviewed below.

As mentioned previously, the forest products industry has taken seriously the possibility that pollutants labeled acid rain might be damaging forests since 1979 when it commissioned its independent research organization, the National Council of the Paper Industry for Air and Stream Improvement (NCASI), to analyze existing scientific information on the possible effects of acid deposition on forests. NCASI published an exhaustive review of all the scientific literature, including completed studies and ongoing research relating to possible effects of acid deposition in forests.[13] At that time, 85 completed studies and 20 ongoing studies were examined. NCASI concluded that "the current state of knowledge does not allow any definitive conclusions to be reached regarding the effects of acidic deposition on forest productivity." Two years later, NCASI published another scientific literature review, this time examining 179 completed studies and 88 ongoing research projects. NCASI concluded that "evidence for damaging effects of acidic deposition on forest productivity has not been conclusively documented under field conditions."[14]

Also in 1983, a survey of member companies turned up no evidence of pollution-related damage on industry forest lands.

INDUSTRY RESEARCH

In 1984, top forestry research scientists from 13 forest products companies were brought together by NCASI to answer questions generated by continued concern about the relationship between acidic deposition and forest health.[15] These forest scientists specifically were asked to determine if there were widespread unexplained cases of tree damage or slowdowns in growth rates in U.S. forests that may be caused by air quality problems.

As part of that effort, the company scientists visited major sites of undiagnosed forest damage. First, they examined the situation in Germany. Originally, the German forest problem was thought to be caused by acidic deposition, but closer analysis now suggests that the problem likely is caused by natural stresses and a much broader category of air pollutants.[16] The most common characteristics of the German decline are thought to be:[17]

1. conifers with varying levels of reduced foliage caused by premature loss of oldest needles;

2. hardwoods with small or irregularly shaped leaves on youngest branches;

3. damaged trees located randomly throughout each forest rather than in groups or clumps;

4. similar damage symptoms on all species;

5. the severity and frequency of damaged trees depends on location, age, and forest development;

6. 80 percent of the damaged trees are more than 60 years old; and

7. less than 6 percent of the damaged trees have symptoms related to any other known causes—for instance, insects and disease.

Unfortunately, none of these characteristics is unique to large-scale forest declines or declines caused solely by air pollution. They are common to most normal tree stresses such as competition, climate, disease, insects, and other factors.

The forest industry scientists also visited the San Bernardino Mountains of Southern California. Research over the past 20 years has shown that high concentrations of ozone have caused damage symptoms that in some ways are similar to those described above for West Germany.[18] Very recently, our industry scientists have noted similar ozone-like damage symptoms in the forests near Houston.

RED SPRUCE DAMAGE

Industry scientists also visited the highly publicized declining red spruce forests in the cloud-covered mountain peaks of New England and the Southern Appalachians.[19] It must be emphasized that the damage there is very different from that in Germany and in the San Bernardino Mountains. The tops of the trees and ends of the branches containing the youngest needles have been killed, and damaged trees are in clumps rather than being randomly scattered. The scientists tend to agree with Dr. Arthur Johnson who, as noted previously, believes this result usually is symptomatic of frost or drought damage. It is possible that the effects of climatic conditions were worsened by the uptake of atmospheric nitrogen compounds that reduced the trees' abilities to withstand high stress conditions. There is no indication that acid deposition has contributed to the problem.

Industry scientists also have examined reports of other unexplained tree damage or radial growth rate declines in the Southeast and elsewhere. Scientists have raised serious questions about the methodology used in these studies but believe that, if there is any merit in the findings, the symptoms likely can be attributed to natural causes such as drought, disease, competition, or other factors.[20]

In sum, over the past four years, scientists in the forest products industry have studied all major forest locations having undiagnosed damage symptoms. Not only were industry scientists unable to conclude that this forest damage is definitely linked to acid rain, but they also could not positively conclude that other specific air pollutants—acting singly or together—were the culprits.

It must be pointed out that, although air quality was not proven to be the primary cause of forest health problems, industry scientists are reluctant to rule it out entirely for some locations. We simply do not have air quality data on forest lands; this lack of air quality monitoring information is gradually being addressed. There are more data today than there were even two years ago. For as noted above, most of the nation's federal, state, and local government air quality monitoring stations are located near urban areas. Those stations in rural or forested areas set up under the federal government's National Acid Deposition Program (NADP) monitor only amounts of acids, nutrients, and other pollutant materials found in "wet deposits." None of the toxic gases, such as ozone, currently are being measured at these sites. (Separate sites have since been set up.)

Because of this paucity of data, industry scientists have recommended a multiyear research plan for the industry that has as its primary goal the determination of ambient air quality in commercial forest lands. Other goals include determining—under experimental conditions—responses of major tree species to ambient concentrations of the most important air pollutants and determining—under "real world conditions"—the effects of air quality for forest lands. The industry set a first-year funding goal of $1.3 million for 1986 and has pledged $1 million a year more as the studies have progressed.

The forest products industry strongly believes that taking the time to carefully perform this needed research is critical. In the few years scientists have been studying the possibility of a cross-media pollution problem—for example, the possible impacts of air pollution on forest health—a number of hypotheses already have been examined and rejected, each of them hailed initially as a solution to the supposed forest health problem. Other hypotheses now have been developed, but they require additional study before we can safely assume that they explain what is happening in the woods.

WRONG SOLUTIONS

If we act on these hypotheses before they are proven, we could embark on costly solutions that may have little, if any, impact on forest health. Worse, from the industry's and—we suspect—the environmental community's point of view as well, if we proceed with the wrong solution, the nation could be lulled into a false sense of security that the claimed air pollution-induced forest health problem, if indeed there is one, already has been fixed and that no further action is necessary. The industry still is not sure that there is a regionwide air pollution problem for forests, although there is increasing concern about ozone.

When ambient air quality levels in forests are known, and when the extent of the effect of air pollutants on trees is determined, then, and only then, will we have a better understanding of whether air quality is adversely affecting our forests—and, most importantly, what, if anything, we need to do about it.

The forest products industry has committed substantial resources to answering questions about the relationship between air quality and forest health. Answers will be found. If action is needed, the industry will act. We submit that is the proper course for dealing with the cross-media aspects of pollution.

NOTES

1. Ellis, Cowling, "Acid Precipitation in Historical Perspective," *Environmental Science and Technology* 16, no. 2: (1982) 110A–123A.

2. H. Seip and A. Tollan, "Acid Precipitation and Other Possible Sources for Acidification of Lakes," *Science of the Total Environment* 10: (1978) 253–270.

3. Acid Precipitation Act of 1980 (Title VII of the Energy Security Act of 1980) 94 Stat. 770, 42 U.S.C. 8901--8905.

4. In the 99th Congress, more than 150 members signed on as cosponsors of H.R. 4567, an acid rain control bill introduced by Reps. Gerald Sikorski (D-Minn.) and Henry Waxman (D-Calif.). This bill passed the House Energy and Commerce Committee's Subcommittee on Health and the Environment 16–7 on May 20, but never passed the full committee. The Senate Environment and Public Works Committee held hearings on S. 2203 and other legislation, but never voted on a bill. Both the House and Senate were expected to resume active consideration of acid rain legislation in early 1987, but as the 100th Congress was ending its session in October 1988, no bills were forthcoming. Meanwhile, several states, including New York, Wisconsin, and Massachusetts, have passed their own acid rain legislation. In the last Congress, the House has been the most active in introducing acid rain legislation. On March 16, 1989, Reps. Gerald Sikorski (D-Minn.) and Silvio Conte (R-Mass.) introduced the Acid Deposition Control Act of 1989, H.R. 1470. This bill is identical to H.R. 4567 introduced in the 99th Congress. In early 1989, H.R. 1470 is still in hearings and is not expected to move rapidly. It does, however, appear to be the strongest piece of acid rain legislation so far. Another notable proposal was introduced by Rep. Jim Cooper (D-Tenn.) on January 3, 1989 (H.R. 144). It contains some of the necessary provisions for the control of acid deposition, but does not appear to have the strengths of H.R. 1470. Other bills on acid rain have been introduced in both the House and the Senate in the 101st Congress, but it is likely little action will be taken on these.

5. J. N. Woodman, "An Industrial Forester's Perspective on Air Pollution and Forest Decline," *Proceedings of Symposium on Effects of Air Pollution on Forest Ecosystems*, Acid Rain Foundation, St. Paul, Minn. May 8–9, 1985.

6. George H. Weyerhaeuser, "Ozone, Not Acid Rain, Main Threat to Forest Growth," *Financier*, December 1985, pp. 34–36.

7. Warren Richey, "Tiny Worm Eating Away at North Woods," *The Christian Science Monitor*, October 3, 1984, p. 3.

8. Harold Faber, "After Lull, Gypsy Moths Strike Northeast," *The New York Times*, October 21, 1985, p. B3.

9. J. E. Pinkerton and A. S. Lefohn, "Characterization of Ambient Ozone Concentrations in Commercial Timberlands Using Available Monitoring Data," *TAPPI Journal* 69, no. 4 (April 1986) 58–63.

10. Arthur H. Johnson and Samuel B. McLaughlin, "The Nature and Timing of the Deterioration of Red Spruce in the Northern Appalachian Mountains," National Research Council, *Acid Deposition Long-Term Trends*, Washington, D.C. (National Academy Press, 1986), pp. 200–230.

11. Jack Horan, "Forest Sleuths Track Mystery of Dying Trees," *The Charlotte (N.C.) Observer*, October 14, 1984, p. 1.

12. Dr. John Barber, executive vice-president, Society of American Foresters, Testimony at oversight hearing before the Subcommittee on Mining, Forest Management, and Bonneville Power Administration of the Committee on Interior and Insular Affairs, U.S. House of Representatives, Washington, D.C., June 7, 1984.

13. National Council of the Paper Industry for Air and Stream Improvement, "Acidic Deposition and Its Effects on Forest Productivity: A Review of the Present State of Knowledge, Research Activities, and Information Needs," Atmospheric Quality Improvement Technical Bulletin No. 110 (New York: 1981).

14. National Council of the Paper Industry for Air and Stream Improvement, "Acidic Deposition and Its Effects on Forest Productivity: A Review of the Present State of Knowledge, Research Activities and Information Needs—Second Progress Report," Technical Bulletin No. 342 (New York: 1983).

15. B. B. Stout, and I. Gellman, "Development and Current Implementation of the Forest Products Industry's Investigative Program on Air Quality and Forest Health," pp. 1–2, Proceedings of the 1986 TAPPI Annual Meeting Atlanta, March 2–5, 1986.

16. B. Ulrich, R. Mayer and P. K. Khanna, "Chemical Changes Due to Acid Precipitation in a Loess-Derived Soil in Central Europe," *Soil Science* 130 (1980): 193–199.

17. P. Schutt and E. B. Cowling, "Symptoms of German Forest Decline," *Plant Disease*, 69: (1985) 548–558.

18. J. R. McBride, P. R. Miller, and R. D. Laven, "Effects of Oxidant Air Pollutants on Forest Succession in a Mixed Conifer Forest Type of Southern California," *Air Pollutants Effects on Forested Ecosystems*, 1985.

19. H. W. Vogelmann, "Catastrophe on Camels Hump," *Natural History*, 91 (1982): 8–14.

20. U.S. Department of Agriculture, Forest Service, "Forest Service Resource Inventory: An Overview," Forest Resources Economics Research Staff (Washington, D.C.: 1982); and Alan Lucier, "Summary and Interpretation of Forest Service Report on Pine Growth Reductions in the Southeast," National Council of the Paper Industry for Air and Stream Improvement, Technical Bulletin No. 508 New York: 1986)

9

Comprehensive Planning and Environmental Ethos

Evan C. Vlachos

ABSTRACT

The emerging planning practice and ethos of the last 15 years have been responses to a series of important transformations including increasing complexity, magnitude of potential impacts, rapidity of change, search for equity, and the demand to cope. These responses emanate also from shifting attitudes toward the environment, broad concerns about the resilience and tolerance of the ecosystem, expanding conceptual and methodological capabilities, and the renewed commitment toward environmental scanning and organizational mobilization. The suggested responses to a transforming society include emphasis on risk management, futuristic posture, prudent reasoning, and contingency planning.

Key Words: social transformations, normative planning, futurism, contingency planning

ENVIRONMENTAL CONSIDERATIONS AND COMPREHENSIVE PLANNING

Voluminous material on population, the ecosphere, and the depletion of natural resources attests to the centrality of the plight of contemporary society with regard to expanding numbers, limitations of space, and the degradation of our living environment. Critical issues in natural resources today are population growth, resource shortages and depletion, spatial imbalances, environmental despoilation, and the limits to human adaptive capability in a technological society. Such concerns—combining aspects of both quantity and quality—tend to reinforce prevailing fears that something fundamental is changing in the relationship between individual and nature. Some scientists even believe that the world's strains today are perhaps signals of an unsolvable crisis, namely the approach of physical limits to human and material growth.

This argument is accentuated by an increased awareness of what the human presence is doing to the surrounding ecosystem and the natural laws concerning young and mature ecosystems. The key question has to do with the tolerance, resiliency, or recuperability of the surrounding environment and reflects concern with the general assimilative capacity of the environment to absorb human intervention or to meet increasing human demands.

There seems to be general agreement that we are passing a phase of a great transformation with potential for further expansion or equally well for catastrophic consequences for our collective life. This period of transformation is characterized by certain broad fundamental changes in our outlook and activity including, among others: exponential changes in technology with incremental changes in social life, need for adaptation, significant social morphological changes, increases in the knowledge capital, and important ideological transformations.

These broad movements of a societal "transition" or "transformation" are also pointing toward the need for a more holistic, interdisciplinary, and systems approach to a complex society; to a growing emphasis on understanding secondary and tertiary effects, thus bringing the future into sharper focus; to a more comprehensive look at nature; and to new outlooks with regard to international interdependencies.

It is not only that technical problems proliferate faster than social solutions can be found to meet them, but also the very quantity of problems changes their qualitative character. Thus, each successive set of new or residual problems is more difficult to solve than predecessor problems.

This rapidly transforming environment is characterized by continuous changes that can be summarized in four major categories:

1. sociocultural changes representing values, norms, and shifting structural features of transforming societies;
2. institutional changes referring to the role that various institutions—most notably the government—play in the planning and management of natural resources;
3. technological changes affecting distribution and utilization of resources through innovative techniques, alternative hardware solutions, or nonphysical solutions to resource problems; and

4. contextual changes involving new patterns of understanding the world around us and knowledge as to critical interrelationships, such as new ecological models and environmental insights—including new epistemological approaches, "soft ecology," the concept of Gaia, "appropriate technology," and so on.

As a result of such forces of change, a series of major transformations has been taking place. Such transformations are particularly relevant to the planning of natural resources and include:

1. Increasing societal complexity that accentuates the interdependence and vulnerability of collective life—with potential institutional gridlock.

2. The magnitude of effects or the intensity, severity, or duration of impacts from man-made interventions that test the tolerance or resiliency of surrounding environments.

3. The rapidity of change often exemplified in the popular term "future shock," which in turn not only creates a bewildering context of fast-changing circumstances, but also shortens the time available for effective decision making.

4. The distribution of effects or the whole question of equity and fair access to resources by all citizens.

5. The demand for coping action or the increasing uneasiness about our reactive approaches to changing circumstances and a commitment to develop more proactive approaches.

These transformations suggest that modern society, because of its size, complexity, diversity, structural differentiation, or environmental alterations, contains a comparatively high amount of potential disorganizational strains and stresses.

Underlying the forces of change and the major transformations outlined above are two central themes: complexity and control. Not only is our society growing more complex and interdependent, but accelerating change—driven primarily by technological breakthroughs—reinforces the need for coping mechanisms. At the end, to be able to understand the structural transformations of the world around us, especially of natural resources, we need appropriate conceptual frameworks and analytic capabilities, methodological tools that will permit us to measure change and chart desirable futures, and normative commitments that would incorporate the goals to be achieved and futures to be created. Such capabilities are necessary if we also observe that mistakes are becoming more costly, there is less forgiving in the environment, and our goals are becoming much more complex given competing and conflicting demands.

THE PRACTICING ETHOS

If one looks back at the last 15 years, quite significant changes characterize the planning and management scene in the context of natural resources development. The exuberance of the early 1970s—with the campaigns to clean the environment, the commitment to comply with the National Environmental Policy Act, and our initial joy of trying to find new tools to measure changes around us—is now becoming a much more reflective and challenging practice in the 1980s.

It is a realism necessitated by political, legal, and cultural changes with an emphasis on productivity, of a changing economy, and by competitions and competitors that we are not accustomed to. This shifting interest finds us also with better data, much more complex models, with improvements in the retrieval of information and modeling—all of which make us somewhat better prepared for accounting for the far-reaching, indirect, cumulative consequences of our actions.

On top of this there exists also a clarion call for more monitoring, auditing, and feedback. Furthermore, we are preoccupied with the notions that time available may be short, that the planning horizon must be expanded to incorporate disciplines and people and items that have not been considered in the past, that all of a sudden from the direct impacts we are moving to the challenging demand to account for cumulative consequences, and that we need to have relevant organizations and institutions in order to achieve implementable action.

Perhaps in a summary fashion we can underline some important aspects of practicing planning and management ethos in four clusters of important trends and developments:

1. New attitudes toward the environment, especially because of developments associated with the environmental movement, changes in the information base, changes in the understanding of environmental systems, and shifts in human responses to the environment.

2. Renewed concerns with regard to the assimilative capacity of the environment, problems of controlling rapid growth, aspects of equity, and underlying concerns with social well-being and quality of life.

3. Expanding methodological capabilities, including more sophisticated complex modeling; extrapolative, normative, and contingency planning; extended planning horizon—in terms of space, time, and severity of effects; forecasting and risk assessment; and decision support systems for more balanced approaches.

4. Organizational mobilization and institutional changes in terms of professionalism, judicial clarification, conflict management, alternative dispute resolution, and administrative improvements.

THE FUTURISTIC STRAIN

Central to these shifts and changes in planning practices has also been the cross-cutting emphasis on "looking forward" and on planning with an eye toward the future. There are essentially two basic directions from which one can approach the future. One may be called the "exploratory" or "extrapolative" approach. Through a historical, predictive model we ask ourselves: What trend or event forecasts can be made with regard to existing social, political, economic, and technological situations?

The second direction may be broadly labeled "normative" or "teleological." It involves preferred futures and a delineation of desired goals and objectives about alternative future worlds that we want to achieve through a conscious process of social change. To put it another way, in exploratory forecasting one moves from the present—with knowledge of the past—toward the future; normative forecasting implies a "backward" move from idealized or desired future states to the present.

We are faced with three general difficulties in forecasting and futurism. One is the underlying flaw of many methods, namely the assumption that the future has many of the characteristics of the present and that it is more or less an extension of the trends of the past—linear thinking and "historicism." The second has to do with the fluidity of change, the contradictory signs, and the ambiguity of baseline developments. Finally, the third revolves around "ideological" approaches and basic images or icons of the future.

The last category of difficulties is of particular importance if we are to understand the current strong debates about the future of natural resources and planning. To put it plainly, there are different clusters of assumptions, methods, and policy implications between the pessimists and the optimists.

The first represent the "gloom-doom" scenarios of impending catastrophes. For the prophets of doom—occasionally labeled as pessimists, technophobes, Cassandras, or catastrophists—in every area from energy to food, from heat to pesticides, from population to resources, time is the big enemy. The more people there are, the more difficult it becomes to propose solutions and the narrower is the difference between success and failure. For such prophets, there is little if anything in the present that can give us hope that things will be better. Even further, technology will accentuate our predicament. The images of the future and the models of the world to come are filled with dire predictions, reverses, shortages, and confrontations.

The other pole—represented by scenarios of "boom-zoom"—reflects the essential optimism of a better future, even if we may have some temporary setbacks. Exponents of this imagery of things to come—

variably called optimists, cornucopians, technophiles, or Prometheans—base their assumptions on the challenge-response notion of history. They are the ones who believe that, in times of severe stress for mankind, science and technology have always found solutions. The "crisis" that we are passing—be it environmental or social—is no different from other crises, even worse crises in the history of humanity—and individuals and societies will rise to the occasion.

These short remarks on different assumptions about the future course or state of events are part of three underlying types of conflicts in approaching our understanding of change and of eventual planning thrusts:

1. Cognitive conflicts: These represent our disagreements about the "facts," the true nature of trends and of the "critical" variables comprising various models—disagreements as to what we know about the past and the present. Here one can find the healthy debates as to data and statistics used, estimates and probabilities, and the extent and reversibility of perceived risks. The resolution of such conflicts is highly dependent on further research as factual differences can be accommodated by advances in knowlege.

2. Stakeholder conflicts: These reflect coalitions of social power and/or "parties-at-interest" or the different perspectives of the question of "who is at stake." Relevant disagreements here relate such important items as equity or who pays and who benefits, aspects of trade-offs including multiobjective planning considerations, and doubts as to representation, that is, the legitimacy of representing particular groups or even society at large.

3. Ideological conflicts: These are the ultimate expression of social values disagreements, visions of society, models of development, and postures toward the present and the future such as optimism versus pessimism. Such conflicts represent not only all-encompassing points of view, but also ideological axes of collecting data, representing solutions, and evaluating planning success.

Such considerations can serve as a backdrop for a more generalized concern with the development of new approaches to assessment, planning, and decision making that would:

1. place emphasis on stronger interdisciplinary approaches integrating a variety of "environments" and disciplines in any assessment effort,

2. underscore the search for a "social calculus" of project effects and the establishment of a wider range of alternatives,

3. expand the time horizon from a narrow enumeration of immediate impacts to a long-range forecasting of higher-order consequences, and

4. combine the historical experience of the past, the constraints of the present, and the visions of both possible and desirable futures.

"Development" and "preservation" are the emerging dual themes of any contemporary discussion of natural resources planning. The remaining unspoiled natural environments have high incremental value to the nation. At the same time, natural resources are needed for continued national economic viability. In addition, present and future problems are accentuated by the fact that, although the nation is rich in natural resources, many of them are to be found in both fragile ecological systems and landscapes highly valued for their undeveloped state—especially in the West, where major tracts of public land still exist. Thus, rapid development and the attractiveness for development of many parts of the nation may impose very high environmental and social costs and have far-reaching consequences. At stake is the totality of an open environment, values contained in the associated natural environments, and a long historical tradition concerning open spaces.

LOOKING FORWARD

Change—perennial change—has been a constant companion of mankind. Conditions are changing fast, political and social institutions are in constant flux, our perceptions of things to come shift with a predominance of negative forebodings, and we are still searching for some utopian harmonious relationship among the individual, the culture, and the environment. If we believe in the notion that we can interact with our destiny, then we must apprehend the forces shaping our future, control drift, and learn how to cope with uncertainty, turbulence, and changing environments.

With regard to planning and natural resources, "final development" is characterized by: (1) a mature resources infrastructure serving a well-developed economy; (2) trends of continuing economic development, resource exploitation, and population growth; and (3) remaining resource alternatives that are becoming more costly, more complex, and environmentally and socially more perturbing with the consequence being that each new type of resource development alternative is characterized by continuous conflict and controversy.

Growth and development as well as continuous change vis-a-vis resources set into motion a variety of cause-effect-cause chains, and trigger a whole interrelated system of impacts and consequences that create new economic and environmental conditions, change the social opportunities for existing population groups, produce new or different services and products, and create new institutional responses to changing and complex circumstances.

Looking backward, there are some hard-earned lessons as how to cope with the future. For example, we have come to recognize that:

1. scarce resources require thoughtful planning,
2. we need to bring together all groups in the form of participatory and anticipatory democracy,
3. what we value can become a rallying point,
4. we must accommodate fundamental shifts in values,
5. contingency planning allows for flexible responses to fast-changing conditions, and
6. while futures cannot be predicted, they can be created.

In trying to describe transforming environments and planning mechanisms, one can adopt three basic postures. The first can be described as the "optimistic posture," which recognizes potential technological breakthroughs, good management, rationality of the system, and a developmental ethos associated with high technology, economic expansion, and mastery of the surrounding environment.

Contrasted to the optimistic school, the "catastrophic preoccupation" envisages negative spillovers, erosion, crowding, and a long-term disastrous drift toward a wholesale destruction of the world around us.

In the midst of these two extremes lies what we may call a "middling" position or a middle-road posture that recognizes some localized disasters but is cautious in both the responses and policies to be adopted by simply maintaining a traditional wisdom approach where some setbacks are also offset by eventual prudent management processes.

Central to these three preoccupations or postures, ranging from highly optimistic through a middle-of-the-road approach to an apocalyptic fascination are such contested issues as the extent of climatic changes, the role of human intrusion—especially urbanization and industrialization, the practices of resource development and use, the overdraft of water, and the extent of energy development. Connected also to the above are such larger concerns and concepts as carrying capacity, tolerance and resilience of the ecosystem, thresholds and trigger points, and—more broadly—the interdependence of resources. Finally, transcending all such discussions are such critical items as available time span for decision making; relevant, valid, and reliable data in order to be able to make proper decisions; and the concern with long-range, interactive, diachronic effects in the interrelationship between population, culture, and the biosphere.

Again, the effort to live with an uncertain future entails, among others:

1. a shift from short-range crisis management to a long-range risk management or a proactive posture,

2. foresight building and capacity toward flexible and extended time horizon planning,

3. structural transformations in our society and major institutional overhaul, and

4. understanding of our cultural metamorphosis in terms of fundamental shifts in social values.

Knowing that we must learn to survive in the context of ambiguity and uncertainty, we are asked to combine diagnosis (problem identification) with prognosis (or alternative futures) and action (or concrete strategies and tactics). Such a synthesis requires an imaginative coalescence of knowledge, prudent judgment, and reasonable implementation options.

An equally important challenge is the strong competition among various areas of the nation. Together with many of the points raised earlier, this situation leads to four interrelated questions:

1. How do we balance in an equitable manner costs and benefits involved in the alteration of the surrounding environment?

2. How do we proceed with planning and appropriate transitions to new states without unacceptable disruptions to our ecosystems?

3. How do we measure or evaluate in a valid, reliable, refined, relevant, and comparable manner intervention effects?

4. How do we implement action or fill the gap between theory and practice?

Our conclusion, then, is not to get entangled in the interminable listing of trends and developments, to project only current trends, or to expand analytical studies continuously. We need a skillful combination of structured reasoning and disciplined imagination. Improving background information; broadening the thought process in terms of uncertainty, probabilities, alternatives, and cross-impacts; adopting an overall posture of tolerance toward ambiguity; and accepting risk and uncertainty as a challenge—all will facilitate the passage toward the future.

In the context of the brief remarks made above, it is imperative that we combine knowledge, judgment, and action. In concrete terms such a combination implies increased capacity for environmental scanning and trend monitoring; decision support systems that can extend data and information to knowledge and, hopefully, wisdom—by adding experience and common sense; organizational mobilization in terms of personnel, facilities, and procedures as well as risk management emphasis; and, once again, contingency planning that would be characterized by a richer menu of options, flexibility, midcourse correctability, and preparedness for alternative choices and action in a surprise-full world.

The adaptation, then, to a new fast-transforming society and the changing planning and environmental ethos requires that we must account for the full range of impacts of our actions, develop plans that can delineate consequences in advance, control events and the environment for the common good, and—last but not least—interact with our destiny so as to be part of it.

NOTE

While this chapter does not contain footnotes and specific bibliographical references, the debt to the existing literature is immense. The following works were particularly useful in the formulation of the above argument: Bill Devall, "The Deep Ecology Movement," *Natural Resources Journal* 20, no. 2 (April 1980): 299–322; Martin W. Holdgate et al., "World Environmental Trends Between 1972 and 1982," *Environmental Conservation* 9, no. 1 (Spring 1982): 11–29; Ernest Patridge, ed., *Responsibilities to Future Generations: Environmental Ethics* (Buffalo, N.Y.: Prometheus Books, 1981); *State of the Environment: An Assessment at Mid-Decade*, a report from The Conservation Foundation (Washington, D.C., 1984).

10

Land Use: What You Need to Know

Norman A. Berg

ABSTRACT

Local jurisdictions primarily control the nation's private land-use system. There are critics of this process. Do local decisions fully represent state and/or national interests? Rural people view land-use issues from a different perspective than those who live and work in cities. They want to be involved in the planning process.

Key Words: land use, regulation, property rights, planning, growth management, decision-making, resource limits, urban expansion, agriculture

BACKGROUND

The general problem of land use has many faces. It is a national concern, and yet for the most part it is a very local concern. It can be a long-range issue, as when planning a new community, or it can be immediate, as evidenced by the need for new waste management sites. In any sense, it is important, and the need for affirmative action is urgent.

Throughout U.S. history, land use has had a strong impact on our destiny. In colonial times, land was used to lure colonists, to pay off political debts, and to establish governments. National land policies have provided homesteads for settlers, lands for railroads, and land-grant colleges to work among the nation's farmers and ranchers. National land policies have also established national forests, parks, wildlife refuges, and grasslands as well as a nationwide soil and water conservation program to protect the U.S. land base.

CURRENT ISSUES

Today, conflicting demands for land resources are placing severe strains on economic, social, and political institutions. Current land-use decisions are making a lasting impact on the natural environment. No area of the country is free from land-use problems, though the shape of these problems often differs from region to region.

Discussions about land use proceed as if there were one set of widely accepted and understood land-use goals. No such agreement is apparent. Citizens group into distinct but polarized camps. Increasingly we see the "I-got-mine" property owners concerned with protecting their own interests, while pretending to work for the good of all. There are also the builders, out to pillage and ravage the land, and the environmentalists who prefer wildlife and serenity to people.

Those who urge new land-use regulation, for example, suggest that access to land should be viewed not as a private right but rather as a public entitlement that accompanies citizenship. They would remove land from the market sector, where it is apportioned according to people's ability and willingness to pay. Instead, they would distribute land services according to public needs. At the other end of the spectrum are those who maintain that the land should be treated like any other privately held commodity, essentially as private property with a minimum of public direction or interference.

Between these poles are those who take the position that private property rights in land exist alongside public entitlements to land, and that a proper weight to the latter requires far more limitations on the former than now exist.

A still different fundamental position emerges from the perspective of some planners who would apportion land uses to particular parcels and regions without reference to the economics of land markets but would rely on such criteria as aesthetics, convenience, urban design, and ecology.

In short, economists, planners, public officials, the business community, conservationists, the courts and the legal profession, and citizens generally seem to be traveling markedly different routes in their approach to the role of land in our society. These differences naturally lead to sharply divergent views on the purposes and nature of land-use planning and implementation.

ROLE OF GOVERNMENT

Control of the nation's private land-use system is overwhelmingly exercised by local jurisdictions. Much criticism over land policies has been directed—right or wrong—at several aspects of this localism: (1)

narrowness of focus, to the neglect of rights and needs of adjacent jurisdictions, the metropolis as a whole, the region, the state, and the national interest; (2) ineptness and conflicts of interests, among officials managing local land-use controls; and (3) the absence of sufficient participation by citizens in land-use decisions that vitally affect their lives.

A broad array of public and semipublic organizations and agencies can become involved in land-use decisions. Many problems go beyond political boundaries, and improved technology enlarges potential service areas. But most local governments have not yet expanded geographically to the point where they can provide such area service. They may possess the technical potential, but their machinery for decision making and coordination may not have kept pace with such potential.

OPTIONS

When we think of land as a resource, there appear to be three basic options for using it. One is to utilize land to satisfy current needs, regardless of whether such use exhausts the resource at the expense of future generations. This use of land is commodity- and profit-oriented; the rate at which the resource is expended depends on consumer demand and on competitive use of other resources.

Another option is to conserve land by using it in a way that maintains or renews the resource, thus giving future generations more options when their turn comes for making land-use decisions. Conservation implies managed land use.

A third option is to preserve the land by leaving it in its natural state, so that future generations may decide whether to exploit, conserve, or preserve land based on their values and needs. The preservation of marshes, wetlands, virgin timber and prairie, and wilderness areas has strong support as public policy. Some combination of these options is another possibility—and may be the answer in many instances.

Land-use planning is neither good nor bad. What it should do is combine technical facts and human preferences into a political process for making important local decisions. The challenge is to work toward a new and more adequate planning process that will reduce community problems while avoiding the injustices of the past. Future problems— environmental, economic, or social—are likely to be more difficult to deal with than those of the past. So any new process that is developed had better be a good one.

A RURAL VIEWPOINT

I confess to a degree of frustration as I attempted to put into words the rural viewpoint on land use. It is true that rural people view land-use issues from a different background from those who live and work in cities. It would be useful to examine a few of the reasons for this.

However, it seems to me that the rural viewpoint is very similar to the urban viewpoint—or to any other viewpoint in this country today. If there is one thing the many land-use controversies have shown, it is that land use does not present a distinctively "urban" or a distinctively "rural" problem. This is one country, and any land-use problem that afflicts the nation must be successfully dealt with in both rural and urban areas. No matter what our individual life-styles may be, we should all want what is best for the country as a whole, as well as for our own particular area. I support one nation—not just a disparate collection of urban boroughs and rural settlements—in my limited efforts to interpret concerns of landowners for their lands.

As we know, land-use planning is historically an urban growth-management tool. It had its roots in the 1920s, as city planners in New York City and other densely populated areas attempted to cope with the growing conflicts among citizens as a result of unguided land-use decisions. One early goal was to keep a slaughterhouse separate from a neighborhood of fine homes. Location of the slaughterhouse as proposed would have resulted in lower property values for homes in that area—in effect, a "taking" of property value from the homeowners by the slaughterhouse owner. In cities and towns today, this is still one basis for land-use planning and control.

Gradually, a zoning tool emerged. Areas were identified and located according to the dominant land use—residential, commercial, industrial, and so on. That is all well and good where much of the development is already in place. An area of homes is likely to remain residential for some time, and zoning it as such causes little difficulty.

New problems crop up, however, when open agricultural land is involved. Who can look at good farmland near a city and say with certainty that it should be houses, or businesses, or factories in 20 years?

There may be some very good reasons why it should be, and the ultimate design of the city might be greatly enhanced if it were, but there are good reasons why it may never happen. Economic conditions change, people's desires change, and opportunities arise that can not be foreseen. Fulfilling the plan's goals may require hundreds—even thousands—of private decisions about investments, sales, developments, and even life-styles. Growth management and land-use controls can attempt to guide these decisions, but certainly can not dictate them. If too many people think the original plan is no longer valid, it will either be ignored or changed.

Farmers, ranchers, and foresters understand this problem. As individuals, many have been planning the use and management of land for a long time. They know that planning is needed—that a good agriculturist does not bend with every breeze. They have planned cropping systems, conservation systems, and management systems of all sorts. But they also understand that the most useful plan is the one that is most flexible—the one that gives them realistic options and that allows them to react to new conditions, make new decisions, seize new opportunities, and avoid new hazards. They are cynical of the ability to fix a firm "plan" for the future and never depart from it. So, to the extent that new land-use planning programs are described as efforts to draw new maps—or make fancier plans—rural people are often skeptical.

Does this mean they oppose necessary land-use regulation and management? Perhaps not. In the past, rural people have led the way in designing community decision-making programs such as those that conserve and help develop land resources. Rural people are still guiding community investment decisions that influence land and water use.

Many other land-use decisions, however, are being made without rural interests at heart. These decisions might involve anything from private profit-making opportunities to greater efficiency in city operations. But more and more farmers are becoming concerned with them. If the outcome of a particular decision-making process is going to affect vital rural interests, then larger numbers of rural people are going to be demanding access to that process.

Many of the new land-use programs springing up in the states recognize this. Very few of them propose new map-drawing or plan-making for the sake of a document. Most concentrate on outlining new decision-making processes that involve both local and state governments. Where these state programs have been designed to give fair consideration to agricultural and forestry interests, to provide the opportunity for rural people to have access to the decision-making process, and to carefully balance the public interest with private rights, they have enjoyed the support of rural people.

Furthermore, farmers, ranchers, and foresters have by necessity thrived on hard work and self-reliance. They have learned how to make daily decisions in a high-risk way of life. Our existing "farm policy" and programs for commodities—prices, acreage, and such—do impact farmers and their decisions. They do not like it, but live with it. Farmers need government, and government needs farmers. It is something of a "shotgun marriage" that will likely persist in some form for major commodities such as wheat, corn, cotton, rice, dairy products, and the like. They do not want to abandon this initiative to some government agency.

Farmers et al. are wary for other reasons as well. As we noted, much of past land-use planning originated in cities, and many farmers have observed these efforts firsthand. In fact, one out of every four farmers is located in a Standard Metropolitan Statistical Area. These people have seen the local planning process result in decisions affecting the value of their land, and perhaps even their ability to stay in business. Often, agricultural values have been lost in the scramble among developers to make the fastest buck possible and in the inability of growing communities to keep on planning and providing services that keep pace with rapidly changing demands. Often, too, farmers have had little— if any—voice in the decision-making process. They have been spectators—not participants. This experience has made rural people look twice at any "plan-drawing" that appears to place rigid guidelines on an uncertain future. They view with suspicion any plan or decision-making process that has a potential for greatly affecting their land without providing a mechanism for protecting their interest.

A COMPLEX PROCESS

The process of land resource use and management is a complex one with many different elements: technical components, broad policy outlines, general plans that have been adapted from earlier experiences. One element present in almost every land-use issue is people.

Successful land-use decisions hinge primarily on people: how well they study the situation, understand the choices, make their preferences known, and indicate their readiness to support the decision. Instead of trying to make choices for people, we would serve them better by designing programs that involve them more extensively throughout the decision-making process. In reaching for more broadly based participation, however, we should not dilute the contributions of local interests.

A trend toward more "people involvement" is already under way. An emerging insistence on "the right to plan" may be the next significant citizen movement in the United States. This should make land-use decisions more generally acceptable once they are made, but it may cause some difficulties in the decision-making process.

IMPORTANT FARMLANDS

An urgent need is to help people understand the problems of resource limits and to make whatever adjustments are necessary to operate within these limits. Prime and unique farmlands are resources in limited supply in the United States. More of this acreage is urbanized every year. About 1.5 million acres of agricultural land—most of that acreage "prime farmland"—are irreversibly removed from production and converted to nonagricultural uses each year. Concerted action is needed to insure that too much of this limited resource is not lost to less vital uses.

Population growth and urban expansion are threatening the best U.S. farmland. A recent study, by the American Farmland Trust (1986), of the top 20 percent of agricultural counties in each state—the high-market-value farming counties—found that over half (58 percent) were either inside or adjacent to a metropolitan area. Some 30 percent of the value of the nation's total agricultural production comes from the high-market-value farming counties located on the rapidly urbanizing fringe of U.S. metropolitan areas. Unless additional measures are taken, including more public direction of land use, much of this irreplaceable farmland will be lost from agricultural uses forever.

As I view the past, it is apparent that some of the clients of the Soil Conservation Service—and of the local conservation districts—with a great deal of clout decided that the SCS had strayed from the role it supported as primarily a "soil erosion" agency. Several efforts—including the gathering of data such as the 1977 and 1982 national resources inventories (USDA 1980, a and b, 1987), support for a national agricultural land study, promoting the defining and mapping of important and unique farmlands, and an effort to improve classification of wetlands—were all actions considered by some in the agriculture business as rights of—and more the turf of—private landowners and users, and certainly not proper roles for SCS. This was especially spotlighted in potential enforcement of the "farmland protection policy" of the 1981 Farm Bill and the efforts to improve USDA soil and water conservation programs pursuant to the Soil and Water Resources Conservation Act of 1977.

Recently, as part of the state of Maryland's initiatives to restore the Chesapeake Bay, the Maryland legislature enacted the Chesapeake Bay Critical Area Law. This new legislation was adopted to minimize the adverse impacts of both point- and nonpoint-source pollutants upon water quality; to conserve fish, wildlife, and plant habitat; and to establish land-use policies for development in the Chesapeake Bay critical area.

This new law created a zone named the "critical area," designated as that portion of land contained within a boundary established 1,000 feet inland from the line of mean high tide of the Chesapeake Bay and its tributaries. Land-use activities within this critical area will be required to comply with criteria established by the Chesapeake Bay Critical Area Commission and the resource protection plans as developed and implemented by the local governments.

As a resident of the state of Maryland for over a quarter of a century, and a participant in land and water conservation programs for that same period at the national level, I have encouraged this latest effort to advance the science and art of good land use at every step. The debate and hearings and points of view were reminders of the long struggle of many to emphasize the need for programs to study and evaluate land-use changes and to report the findings. These activities are still required, but we also need action programs that are politically acceptable and technically workable, by: (1) informing, educating, and involving more people in land-use decisions, and (2) demonstrating that land-use programs can succeed.

SUMMARY

Many issues influence landowners' decisions about how land is used. In rural areas, where land is primarily used for agriculture, the planning for future use needs to include farmers, ranchers, and foresters. Local jurisdictions of government usually control the process of determining land-use policy. Urban expansion threatens the best U.S. farmland, and what happens to our farmland is a national issue. Decisions, for the proper long-term use of all land—rural, urban, private or public—will increasingly determine the quality of life for every citizen. One needs to know more about the system and be a participant wherever one lives and works.

BIBLIOGRAPHY

American Farmland Trust. 1986. "Farming on the Fringe." Maps and Analysis. Washington, D.C.

U.S. Department of Agriculture. 1980a. *Soil, Water, and Related Resources in the United States: Status, Condition, and Trends—Appraisal I.* Washington, D.C.

———. 1980b. *Soil, Water, and Related Resources in the United States: Analysis of Resource Trends—Appraisal II.* Washington, D.C.

———. 1987. *Soil, Water, and Related Resources on Nonfederal Land in the United States: Analysis of Condition and Trends—The Second RCA Appraisal.* Washington, D.C.

11

Innovative Process and Inventive Solutions: Nuclear Waste Packaging Facility Case Study

Elizabeth Peelle

ABSTRACT

A joint Oak Ridge–Roane County, Tennessee, citizen task force evaluated the U.S. Department of Energy's (DOE) proposal to site a monitored retrievable storage (MRS) facility in Tennessee in terms of environmental, transportation, and socioeconomic impacts. Another potential host area rejected the proposal before studying it.

The case study examines how the task force used mitigation, compensation, and incentives (economic and noneconomic) to address the problem of distrust of DOE and to change the net local impact balance from negative to positive. Intensive group interaction during their investigations and development of trust within the task force led to consensus decisions on safety and conditional acceptance. DOE accepted most of the task force's conditions after informal negotiations. The siting process was stopped in 1985 by extensive statewide opposition resulting in legal challenge by the state and vetoes by the governor and state legislature. The Nuclear Waste Policy Act Amendments of 1987 nullified DOE's proposed siting of the MRS in Tennessee and required DOE to begin the MRS siting process anew after receiving the 1989 report of a specially created MRS Review Commission.

Key Words: incentives, compensation, mitigation, negotiation, consensus, siting of noxious facilities, conditional acceptance, distrust, citizen task force, Nuclear Waste Policy Act, Monitored Retrievable Storage, local cost/benefit balance, high-level nuclear waste, safety preconditions for siting

INTRODUCTION AND OVERVIEW

Nuclear waste management facilities are the most difficult of potentially noxious facilities to site. In fact, increasingly sophisticated and widespread public opposition has made problematic the siting of any large industrial or power facility (O'Hare et al., 1983). Despite regional or national benefits, negative local impacts and absence of local benefits usually lead to intense local opposition—the "not-in-my-backyard" phenomenon (O'Hare, 1977; Armour 1984). Proposed ways around the NIMBY impasse for siting hazardous waste facilities include public participation, negotiation, mediation, compensation, mitigation, and other incentives (see, for example, Carnes et al., 1983; Sorensen et al., 1983; and Peelle and Ellis, 1986). Others see the "confidence gap" or public loss of faith in both public and private institutions as the main cause of siting disputes (Hirschhorn, 1984).

The innovative institutional arrangements and possibilities for state and local benefits permitted in the Nuclear Waste Policy Act of 1982 (NWPA) have never been fully implemented. Changes in the NWPA amendments of 1987 are briefly evaluated in terms of local host areas and the work of the MRS task force. This case study reviews the local siting process including negotiation between a potential host area and the U.S. Department of Energy over a proposed monitored retrievable storage facility in the Roane County portion of Oak Ridge, Tennessee, in 1984–86.

We focus upon the intensive process by which a local task force (TF) made the decision about safety, evaluated impacts upon the city and county, and specified conditions needed to change the net benefit balance from negative to positive. Unprecedented positive relationships with the local DOE office permitted productive negotiations over the conditions that the TF felt were necessary for local acceptance. We examine the effects of participation upon the TF as well as the DOE response to the TF proposals for conditional acceptance of the MRS.

However, local acceptance does not a siting make; widespread public and political opposition to the proposed siting developed quickly in the rest of the state, leading to eventual rejection of the MRS proposal by the governor and legislature of Tennessee. We trace briefly the favorable local climate and negative reactions to the MRS and the TF report outside the local area, and draw conclusions concerning the significance and limitations of the TF acceptance.

This particular siting effort was, of course, related to the intense national NIMBY situation in 1984–86 with permanent geological repositories. Half the states made vigorous efforts to avoid selection as DOE sought to fulfill NWPA mandates and site one or two high-level nuclear waste repositories.

WHAT IS AN MRS?

As proposed by the DOE in early 1985, a monitored retrievable storage facility would be an integral part of the national radioactive waste management and disposal system. An MRS would receive, repackage, consolidate, and temporarily store spent fuel from nuclear reactors prior to shipment to a permanent repository. By reducing the total volume and number of shipments, the total number of cask-miles to a repository would be reduced. DOE argued that performing the repackaging and consolidation functions away from a repository would be more efficient and effective, introducing needed flexibility into the waste management system (DOE, 1985b). For alternative views on need for an MRS, see a supporting evaluation as "probably necessary" by the Office of Technology Assessment (1985) and an opposing one by Colglazier (1986).

An MRS program would cost about $2 billion and employ about 700 people. Spent fuel shipments from reactors to the MRS facility would amount to about five trucks per day and ten trains per month. Shipments to the repository from the MRS would involve only two or three unit trains per month. All spent fuel from eastern reactors—about 85 percent of the total—would pass through a Tennessee MRS (DOE, 1986).

METHODS

Information for this study was collected in three ways: (1) direct observation as participant-observer within the socioeconomic subgroup (SEG) of the TF, (2) detailed interviews of 13 of the 31 TF members, and (3) review of written information from the TF, DOE, state of Tennessee, state newspapers for a 12-month period beginning in April 1985, and other sources such as proponent and opponent groups. To check for possible selection bias, all six Oak Ridge volunteers for the TF who were not selected were also interviewed.

The information gained and hypotheses formed by participant observation were tested and revised through intensive interviews. The author participated in most SEG and TF meetings. Interview questions sought to elicit member experiences and views from a sampling of all TF study groups and the executive committee, Roane County and Oak Ridge participants, and technical and nontechnical participants.

WHAT HAPPENED IN THE TASK FORCE?

This section describes what happened during the process of local evaluation of the DOE proposal to site an MRS facility at one of two proposed sites on the Oak Ridge DOE reservation. We review the appointment, scope, and operation of the joint Clinch River MRS task force, interactions within and among study groups, how they arrived at decisions on safety and acceptability, the issues and recommendations developed by the TF, and the goal of consensus.

Formation and Appointment of the Clinch River MRS Task Force

Upon hearing of DOE's decision to site the proposed MRS in Tennessee, it was decided after consultation among state, county, and city officials that a broad citizen effort would be required to evaluate the MRS proposal. A joint proposal for a $100,000 city-county assessment was funded by the Tennessee Department of Health and Environment from the $1.4-million DOE assessment grant to the state. Staff support and fiscal administration were provided by the city of Oak Ridge.

The Clinch River MRS Task Force consisted of three study groups and an executive committee. The study groups evaluated environment and safety hazards, transportation impacts, and socioeconomic impacts. Each study group included an Oak Ridge City Council member, a Roane County commissioner, and three citizens from each jurisdiction. The executive committee consisted of the mayor of Oak Ridge, the Roane County executive and his assistant, and the Oak Ridge city manager and assistant city manager. The latter also served as coordinator.

Appointments of 31 persons to the TF were made in July 1985 by the Oak Ridge City Council after reviewing resumes submitted by volunteers and by the Roane County executive. Of these, 11 were current or former elected officeholders, and nine were employees of Martin Marietta Energy Systems, the prime DOE contractor and operator of the three Oak Ridge DOE installations. No one was directly employed by DOE or the MRS program. About one-third were women.

About half of the TF members had technical—though not necessarily nuclear—training, in line with the city council view that assessing the MRS was primarily a technical task. The group included four engineers, three physicists (one of whom was a health physicist and two with ecology training), a geologist, several housewives with part-time jobs, a statistician, an economist, two real estate or economic developers, a community college administrator, the city fire chief as nonvoting staff support, a county civil defense manager, a county road supervisor, a state highway engineer, president of the League of Women Voters, and a nutritionist. Three could be considered technical "insiders" because of their nuclear waste and transportation expertise.

Task Force Scope and Operations

In order to influence the DOE submission to Congress on the MRS, the TF set a three-month deadline and limited its scope to local impacts. It focused first upon the safety and then the acceptability of MRS operational and transportation impacts upon the social and economic structures of the city and county. The TF initially expected that the state would assess impacts everywhere else in the state; when it became obvious that this was not the case, the transportation study group (TransG) expanded its geographic scope from five to seven counties and made some state-level recommendations. Whether an MRS was needed was considered to be a national rather than local issue and was excluded from TF analysis.

Faced with a huge and difficult task, each study group set up a heavy schedule of study, investigation, public input, discussion, and writing. As illustrated in Figure 11.1, the TF gathered information in many ways and from a large variety of sources. Meetings were held at least weekly, often lasting several hours or all day. Except for the melding of group reports into a final report, most substantive work was done in study groups. Monthly TF meetings were devoted mostly to intergroup communications and logistical planning, as for a western field trip. All meetings were open to the public and attended by local and regional news media. Weekly minutes and additional materials were widely distributed externally upon request.

Concentrating upon the safety and adequacy of technologies to be employed at the MRS, the environmental study group (EnvirG) focused upon worker and public health impacts and possibilities of environmental contamination. This group also attempted comprehensive definition of public concerns and appropriate mitigations.

Initially viewing transportation safety as the key to public acceptance of the MRS, the TransG focused upon safety issues in detail. It used brainstorming to define issues for further study and developed mission and purpose statements. A major effort was preparing a day-long public workshop on nuclear transportation issues. This made TransG the focus of both local and national opponents—Tennessee Valley Energy Council, Sierra Club, and Environmental Policy Institute—who asked for program space for their own experts. When offered roles as resource people but not as speakers, opponents refused to attend a "stacked meeting." Major media attention was focused upon this conflict, opponent opinions, and alleged conflicts within the study group. Few people outside the TF attended the workshop. Except for the *Roane County News*, the media ignored the speakers and substantive content, reporting only the opinions of the few outside attendees.

Figure 11.1
Task Force Information Resources

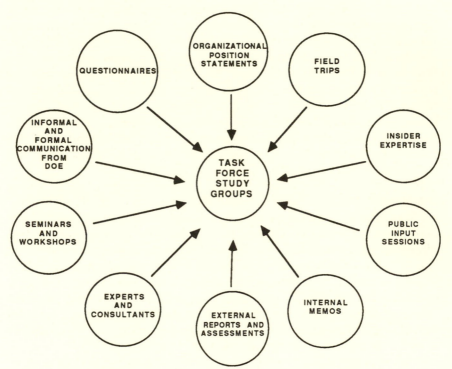

Source: Suggested and designed by John H. Reed (1986).

Focusing upon local social and economic impacts, the socioeconomic group sought to define and ameliorate the many adverse effects it identified. SEG reviewed expectations of local real estate, commercial and tourism developers and investigated impacts at surrogate sites such as nuclear power plants. Several members interviewed local officials at the Barnwell, South Carolina, low-level nuclear waste disposal facility and the Morris, Illinois, spent-fuel storage facility. Unlike the other two groups, an outside consultant was hired to draft the group's report.

Making the Decision about Safety

All study groups viewed safety as a nonnegotiable precondition for acceptance, as per the arguments of Carnes et al. (1983). Safety was addressed directly by two groups. The third—the socioeconomic group—conducted its analysis on the assumption that the MRS would be safe; its chairperson repeatedly stated that SEG would vote for rejection if the findings of the other two groups were negative on safety. Thus, each TF member was implicitly required to come to a decision about the safety and then the acceptability of the proposed facility. This distinction was implicit since both subjects were being investigated simultaneously. The decision involved a complex process of personal study and inquiry, in combination with group and interpersonal interaction; the process developed trust and led to the final consensus on safety.

An intense spirit of inquiry and investigation developed among the entire TF, especially among the two groups studying safety. Members engaged in intensive study of documents, circulation of internal concerns, questioning of each other, and constant discussion in formal and informal settings. "We became good at the continuing process of asking questions," said one. The 69 formal written questions addressed to DOE were one result. Several members commented with satisfaction upon the "let the chips fall where they may" approach. No one interviewed, including the coordinator, reported any interference or suggestions from city or county officials. One member reported initial concern that important questions might go unexamined, and a sense of relief that nothing new turned up in public comments and criticism following release of the TF report. "The questions we asked ourselves were a lot harder than those asked of us by the Tennessee Valley Energy Coalition (TVEC)," said one. "This was the most objective and hard-working group I've ever worked with," said a TF member who had initially opposed the idea of an MRS.

Interaction among technical and nontechnical members was another key to the TF consensus decision upon safety. All but one of the nontechnical members interviewed reported good interaction between themselves and technically trained members. That exception involved an insider who reportedly belittled certain questions. One nontechnical member was initially skeptical of hidden agendas of the technical insiders but eventually appreciated most points raised. "I had to do my homework first and ask lots of questions before I understood," said one member. Many nontechnical people reported strenuous efforts to comprehend their task and the attendant technical material. "I felt better when I found I could ask any question of [three people] in my group. They helped me a lot and never talked down to us. They were looking for answers, too," reported one member. Another did not attempt to conquer the material but supported opponents in being heard before the study group.

Investigative trips undertaken by the TF offered important opportunities to question directly various outside authorities on safety matters. These trips also shaped group members' acceptance of each other, and helped to forge a group identity. The trips to Morris, Illinois, Barnwell, South Carolina, and to western DOE sites involved long hours in transit, concentration upon MRS matters, isolation from competing time demands, and extended after-hours discussion. On the western trip, more doubts surfaced, and more questions were formulated as the members of the two safety groups came to know each other better. Said one member: "We worked in pairs and groups. Answers had to be satisfactory to both types [technical and nontechnical]." Several mentioned this trip as being most influential on their decision that the MRS could be safely operated. According to one member: "My doubts were resolved by seeing the technical processes in operation on the field trip." Another said that "I got answers to my questions on feasibility [of MRS operations] on that trip."

Trust among members developed as a result of the intensive interaction and shared responsibility. One said that "group interactions were most significant in influencing me (regarding the safety decision). All in our group were concerned for the understanding of each person." Each became accepted and respected for his or her individual contribution, effort, capability, and participation in the TF's heavy responsibility for making decisions about safety. Trust grew among TF groups; an SEG member said of the safety groups, "If they are working as hard as we are, they'll flush it out."

By the end, all members were convinced that the MRS could be operated safely and that their safeguards—citizen review board, citizen environmental monitoring, and "gold star" transportation inspections—would help assure its safe operation over time. The intensive information-seeking and evaluation process and the group interaction appear to be the primary contributors to the safety consensus. Though TF members entered with different backgrounds, knowledge, and attitudes toward the MRS, all reached consensus that the MRS could be safe and thus could become acceptable for siting in Oak Ridge if appropriate conditions were added.

Local Issues and Mitigating or Compensatory Conditions

While the other groups were concentrating upon making the decision about safety, the socioeconomic group was discussing what could be done about various negative impacts they foresaw if the MRS were sited and built in Roane County. Following presentation by its consultants, the group adopted its own mitigation-compensation-incentives framework and began developing specific measures to deal with negative economic and social impacts. The principal compensatory measure of importance to the SEG was the full taxability of the facility as if it were privately owned, and as provided for repositories in the NWPA. SEG saw this as the key to preventing the MRS from becoming a local economic burden. A further concern was whether NWPA impact assistance and compensation applied to the MRS since the act does not address these issues adequately for an MRS.

Other major concerns of the SEG were pre- and postoperational negative effects upon local efforts to attract new residents and nonfederal industries. Since diversifying the local economic base and reducing dependence upon federal employment are major local goals, several compensatory measures were devised to offset possible negative effects.

Conditional acceptance of the MRS was a possibility discussed from the first meeting when the TF coordinator broached the subject. The TransG included conditions for safe transport of spent fuel in its early handout sheet. In a formal vote, the SEG decided that the issue was not one of deciding yes or no, but of specifying under which conditions, if any, the MRS would be acceptable to the host area. SEG concluded that, without conditions, the MRS was unacceptable.

Only the EnvirG prioritized the conditions it recommended. Management and other safety-related conditions were given highest priority, while standard environmental impacts[1]—such as construction noise, dust, and blasting impacts—were given lowest priority: "important enough to require mitigation typical of any industrial construction project."

Interactions Among Study Groups

The EnvirG interacted with the other study groups about overlapping concerns. For instance, on the issue of preventing the MRS from becoming a de facto permanent repository, EnvirG's more detailed conditions superseded those of SEG. Both groups developed conditions to meet the concerns of homeowners outside of Oak Ridge directly across from the preferred Clinch River site. Noise, dust, well water, and groundwater concerns were dealt with by EnvirG, while financial concerns were addressed by SEG via the property value insurance recommendation. In another case, both groups recommended local environmental monitoring and a local oversight-control board, but from different approaches: SEG addressed the widespread local distrust of DOE and fears of loss of control over the future, while EnvirG addressed safety concerns and tried to assure continuing management accountability and alertness. Both groups decided that increased local control would help alleviate these concerns.

EnvirG and TransG disagreed over the handling of low level radioactive waste (LLW) from the MRS and proposed studies of ruptured fuel cask impacts. The view of EnvirG prevailed on the LLW issue: shipping it out of Tennessee along with the repackaged spent fuel from the MRS. However, the ruptured cask studies desired by the EnvirG were never approved by the TF. These were the only issues on which consensus was not reached. In both cases, insiders played major roles.

The Goal of Consensus

In addition to the consensus achieved on safety questions, the TF achieved consensus on the conditions needed for acceptability. Though not discussed explicitly, all study groups operated on the principle of achieving a result with which all could agree. Following intensive discussion within study groups of their own recommendations, each group's report was scrutinized by the TF as a whole in an 11-hour session. Examples of issues discussed include the detailed format of the citizen review board and disposition of the LLW. Specific wordings were argued in detail in order to reach a mutually agreeable meaning.[2] In the end, members expressed considerable satisfaction with the result and the process of citizen review. Initial doubts and skepticism were changed by the processes of information gathering, review, and analysis; by setting conditions for siting; and by intensive group interactions and consensus-building. All TF members voted to accept the final report.

DOE INTERACTIONS WITH THE TASK FORCE AND RESPONSE TO THE TASK FORCE REPORT

Task force members expressed surprise over DOE's responsiveness to TF questions and interests. Perceptions of past DOE indifference to local concerns and the lengthy, acrimonious record of in-lieu-of-tax "negotiations" with the city and counties had left a different impression. This time, however, there were early and repeated public statements by officials of DOE's Office of Civilian Radioactive Waste Management (OCRWM) that they would: (1) agree to tax equivalency payments on the entire MRS facility as if it were a private facility and (2) deal constructively and responsively with TF concerns. This change in DOE attitudes is attributed to DOE's response to the new consultation and cooperation (C and C) provisions of the NWPA and to the new head of OCRWM. TF members retained a certain skepticism, however, waiting to see how lasting the DOE attitude change would be, wondering if it would permeate the DOE bureaucracy beyond the MRS staff, and waiting to see how verbal commitments were translated into action and guaranteed arrangements.

The Informal Negotiation Process

Extensive personal contact and active discussion between the newly created local MRS office and TF members developed into an informal negotiation process. DOE personnel and contractors regularly attended study group meetings and were available for questions and discussions. The coordinator had daily phone contacts with the local MRS manager about TF questions and mitigation-compensation proposals. The MRS manager forthrightly discussed DOE's problems and limitations in responding to TF ideas and requests. He tried without success to dissuade the group from submitting certain proposals that he felt DOE or the MRS office could not implement—for example, the citizen oversight board and linkage of MRS construction schedules with those of environmental cleanup of the Oak Ridge reservation. TF members repeatedly expressed their goals but stressed their flexibility about means to these ends.

In this iterative, interactive, and informal fashion, TF proposals as well as DOE responses were shaped. Everyone had a fairly good idea of what might be acceptable to DOE as the process unfolded. Likewise there were no surprises for DOE by the time the TF report was completed. All compensation and mitigation ideas had been discussed throughout with DOE in this informal manner. TF leaders were also pleased with DOE's major effort to provide requested information in a timely manner.

Testing DOE's Good Faith

The first test of DOE's new cooperative attitude came with the MRS environmental assessment (EA) written by a distant DOE contractor (DOE, 1986). No mention was made in the EA of the TF assessment or of DOE's commitments to meet local problems and TF concerns. The EA considered only standard socioeconomic impacts, ignoring nonstandard impacts that comprised the bulk of the TF analysis. In addition, there were numerous factual errors.

SEG reviewers complained loudly because they knew the legal importance of impact documents as a basis for congressional action. TF members wondered publicly if they had been wise in ignoring advice of opponents not to trust DOE. Local DOE officials assured the TF coordinator, however, that the EA would be revised, taking into account TF comments; and it was.

DOE's Formal Response

DOE's formal response to the TF report, therefore, was viewed as the acid test of DOE's verbal pledges and informal agreements. In an unusual move, DOE responded to TF urging and agreed to early TF review of its draft proposal to Congress. This proposal revealed DOE's acceptance in some form of most of the major conditions proposed (DOE, 1987).

Significant differences between the DOE and TF reports involved the composition and power of the citizen review board, property value insurance, and a linkage of DOE reservation cleanup schedules with MRS construction schedules. Significant agreements included tax equivalency payments beginning with authorization of the MRS, the transportation mitigations, limiting MRS storage capacity to 15,000 tons of uranium, and precluding acceptance of any waste by the MRS prior to that time when construction authorization for the first repository is given by the Nuclear Regulatory Commission (NRC).

Many DOE proposals required state agreement for full implementation. This concerned local leaders, who did not share DOE's assumption that vital local conditions would be adequately fulfilled through negotiation of the C and C agreement between state and DOE officials. A detailed comparison of task force conditions and DOE responses is shown in Table 11.1. For another view of the TF effort and its outcome so far as the TF coordinator was concerned, see King (1986).

The Unfinished Negotiation

The TF responded with a detailed letter to OCRWM in January, commending DOE for its responsiveness and reiterating points they felt still needed attention. They accepted in principle DOE's broader MRS Steering Committee, providing that local representation was increased and a majority of the appointees were from Tennessee (Clinch River MRS, 1986).

With the successful legal action initiated by the state of Tennessee in January 1986, this iterative negotiation process (DOE, 1987) ceased. DOE was enjoined from presenting the MRS proposal to Congress until the adequacy of DOE's siting process for the MRS (DOE, 1985a) is reviewed. These same points reappeared in the Nuclear Waste Policy Act Amendments of 1987 wherein Congress nullified DOE's MRS siting proposal and required a new DOE siting effort. The MRS was closely linked in schedule and capacity with the single underground repository effort in Nevada.

LOCAL CLIMATE AND OUTSIDE REACTIONS TO THE MRS AND TASK FORCE REPORT

Supportive Local Area Shows Some Ambivalence

While most people in Oak Ridge and Roane County were favorable toward the possibility of siting the MRS, there was reluctance as well as some organized opposition.[3] A public opinion poll of Oak Ridge sponsored by the local newspaper showed 68 percent in favor of siting the MRS there, 17 percent opposed, and 15 percent with no opinion. The Roane County Chamber of Commerce voted unanimously in favor of the TF report, but the Oak Ridge Chamber delayed its endorsement while debating concerns that an MRS would hinder Oak Ridge efforts to diversify its federally dominated industrial base. Strong support for the MRS as qualified by the TF conditions came from various local community and technical organizations, unions, three local governments, and five local newspapers. Two Roane TF members reported significant anti-MRS feedback, while several Oak Ridge members reported some negative feedback. Both opposition and reluctance were stronger outside the city.

In both jurisdictions, official attitudes followed the pattern of being more favorable than those of the general public. For another example, see Bronfman (1977). For instance, both the Oak Ridge City Council and the Roane County Commission voted unanimously in favor of the conditional MRS task force report, and the mayor of Oak Ridge made strongly pro-MRS public statements throughout.

Other Bases of Local Support

In the face of recent federal cutbacks and job losses, both officials and the general populace were highly sensitive to potential advantages of the MRS such as new jobs and increasing and stabilizing the small tax base remaining outside the nontaxable federal installations. Furthermore, 40 years of federal nuclear research and development and current employment of 17,000 have resulted in general local acceptance and knowledge of nuclear-related activities. Some residents believe that it is Oak Ridge's destiny and responsibility to show the way in safe and exemplary development of new nuclear projects—such as a now-defunct Clinch River breeder reactor or waste management processes and techniques such as the MRS.

Former Oak Ridge National Laboratory director Alvin Weinberg argued, for instance, that the nation must start on something positive in nuclear waste management, that the MRS would provide practice in handling spent fuel and in developing the intragovernmental arrangements needed before a repository is opened, and that the MRS siting was an opportunity for DOE to earn the trust of host communities. The adverse nationwide impact on nuclear waste siting of an Oak Ridge refusal to accept the MRS was also discussed locally.

The only local advocacy group formed was the MRS Information Group, a small ad hoc assemblage of local scientists, engineers, union

Table 11.1

Comparison of Clinch River MRS Task Force Conditions and DOE Response

Task Force Conditions	DOE Response
Tax equivalency payments beginning with authorization of MRS.	Accepted. Binding conditions in C and C agreement on valuation formulas, mediation board for disputes.
Local citizen oversight/ review board with power to stop accepting waste if pre-agreed standards are not met.	State-level Steering Committee (two local and seven other state, public, industry, and DOE representatives). Powers limited to review and suggestion. Chairmen named by DOE in consultation with governor.
C and C agreements between DOE and local governments in MRS authorizing legislation.	Only state-DOE consultation and cooperation (C and C) agreements discussed.
Property value insurance for nearby residents.	Not mentioned.
Mitigate economic development impacts by payments, contractor proximity, location of related private-sector activities, and training programs in local educational institutions. Local procurement requirement.	Mitigation payments. Related activities in private sector. Contractor proximity to be selection factor. Training programs through state and local educational institutions. Existing federal procurement provisions.
Diversification of local industrial base.	Will take appropriate actions to encourage diversification.
Location of ancillary DOE and MRS support activities in Oak Ridge.	Place civilian radwaste transportation system management and new transportation operations and research center at Oak Ridge.
Replace loss of CRBR industrial site.	If land becomes excess to DOE needs.

Table 11.1 (continued)

Task Force Conditions	DOE Response
Tourism impacts.	Mitigation payments.
Public education program on MRS facility, existing DOE programs, and DOE cleanup.	Mitigation payments for MRS only. American Museum of Science and Energy and exhibits and information for MRS only.
Aesthetic appearance of MRS.	Accepted.
Visitor center at facility.	Accepted.
Highway improvements.	To be addressed in C and C agreement. DOE to work with state and local representatives to identify other improvements needed.
Emergency response training and funding.	Assistance to state for adequate capability, equipment, and training. DOE to work with state to develop training standards, will ensure comprehensive training program.
"Gold Star" transportation inspections.	Funding for comprehensive state inspections of spent-fuel shipments arriving and leaving.
Other transportation issues: escorts, methods, indermodal transportation, speeds, and preferred routes.	To be addressed in C and C agreement and in nationwide consultations.
Linkage of DOE cleanup schedule for Oak Ridge reservation with MRS construction schedule.	No commitment made. Explanation of status, plans of current joint cleanup task force (DOE, EPA, state). DOE committed to cleanup as soon as funding and agreement on techniques available.

Table 11.1 (continued)

Task Force Conditions	DOE Response
Complete decontamination and decommissioning of site for unrestricted use at end of life.	Accepted.
Low-level waste shipped out of state.	Low-level waste shipped off site.
Preventing a permanent MRS: Only 300 tons accepted before repository licensed.	No waste accepted until NRC construction license for repository.
Limit storage capacity to 15,000 tons.	Accepted.
Overdue storage penalty.	Not mentioned.
Limit storage to 10,000 tons before outshipments begin.	Not mentioned.

Sources: Adapted from DOE (1987) and Clinch River MRS (1985).

members, and businesspeople. They responded to anti-MRS efforts with a speakers' bureau, letters to newspapers, and information sheets.

Distrust of DOE a Major Source of Opposition

A major source of local and regional opposition to the MRS proposal was distrust of DOE following media revelations of pollution problems on the Oak Ridge reservation. Millions of pounds of mercury and significant amounts of uranium have been lost from DOE facilities to the environment in past decades, but DOE denied the existence of such problems until recently. Though federal cleanup of these and other pollution problems is now proceeding under current federal policy and new local DOE management, there remains significant doubt and skepticism concerning DOE's ability to fulfill agreements and be a good corporate citizen.

Local opposition was led by the TVEC, which organized appearances at several TF meetings to present its views. About a dozen letters of opposition appeared in Oak Ridge and Roane County papers. TVEC members attacked the integrity of TF members, asserting they were "bought" by DOE.

State-Level Opposition Quickly Politicized

Widespread opposition to the proposed MRS siting developed quickly in the state and region. A commissioner of the Tennessee Public Service Commission (PSC) began his unsuccessful campaign for governor with a "Don't Dump on Tennessee" tour in a semitrailer truck. A petition campaign produced 102,000 opposition signatures. A coalition of 17 environmental and other organizations spoke at hearings and protested to the legislature and governor. Among the media, opposition was led by the major Nashville newspaper with antinuclear cartoons and headlines about "the nuclear dump." At a state legislative hearing, TF members were labeled "DOE stooges" and the western trip "a boondoggle." By late fall, the uproar had led to opposition statements from all 11 of Tennessee's U.S. Representatives and most of the Tennessee House and Senate members.

Meanwhile, the state organized an MRS hotline; callers were 90 percent opposed. University of Tennessee researchers found different results in their statewide poll: 58 percent were opposed to an MRS in Oak Ridge, while 62 percent opposed an MRS in Morgan County.

The principal opposition issues were that an MRS was not needed, that transportation and handling were dangerous and exposed Tennesseans to unnecessary risk, anger that all three proposed sites were in Tennessee, distrust of DOE and its record of pollution at Oak Ridge, and that negative perceptions of a nuclear dump would harm state industrial development and tourism.

Opposition at Third Candidate Site

Immediate opposition was also expressed by local officials at the third proposed MRS site in Hartsville, Tennessee. They formed a local evaluation committee similar to one created earlier to deal with impacts at the same site for four—now abandoned—Tennessee Valley Authority (TVA) nuclear reactors. Reluctant at even being involved in the evaluation process, they declared that their citizens would be opposed to any further nuclear projects (Five County REAL, 1985). Hartsville evaluation funds were spent on outside contractors and a telephone poll of citizen opinions, which found that 89 percent were opposed.

Some Task Force Recommendations Adopted by the State

Despite the state of Tennessee's negative orientation toward the MRS and its refusal to agree to Oak Ridge and DOE urging to develop its own mitigation and compensation plan, the TF report was influential with some state agencies. Transportation and environmental conditions in the report were adopted by the state Department of Transportation, the Radiological Health Division, and PSC in their MRS reports to the Governor's Safe Growth Council.

While opposing an MRS in Tennessee, both U.S. Senator Albert Gore, Jr. and U.S. Representative Marilyn Lloyd endorsed the TF report and discussed the need to work for conditions omitted from DOE's proposal in case of a Congressional override.

Governor Opposes MRS for Economic Reasons

The tide of opposition crested in January 1986 with the governor's declaration of opposition. He praised the TF and agreed that safety was no longer a question following favorable findings by state agencies and contractors. But he stated that no MRS was needed and that a siting in Oak Ridge would damage the area's industrial development and tourism because of negative perceptions of nuclear waste.

A Fourth MRS Site Volunteers

To everyone's surprise, officials of neighboring Morgan County then expressed interest in hosting an MRS. They proposed a siting with all the TF conditions and some additional ones tailored to their under-developed and high unemployment area.

Outside support for an Oak Ridge MRS and/or the TF report has been limited to a few state legislators from the area, one national newspaper (USA Today, 1986), various utility and nuclear industry organizations, and OCRWM officials who have praised the report as "a class act."

EFFECT OF PARTICIPATION UPON TASK FORCE MEMBERS

Several months after the conclusion of official TF operations, 13 of the 31 members were interviewed extensively as to their opinions and evaluations about selected aspects of their TF experience. From this information, we evaluated their expectations and the effect of partici-pation upon members.

Half of those interviewed believed that about as much had been done as could be done about gathering public input, given the short time and unchanging opponent questions. The other half believed that public input was inadequate and was a TF failure.

The effect of the intensive participation and study upon members included changing the opinions of a significant fraction of TF members, developing a sense of pride about their participation and achievements, and achieving consensus not only about safety but also about the conditions of acceptability of the proposed MRS facility. The TF developed its own identity, assuming a life of its own independent of its creators. Initial opinions of those interviewed about the safety and feasibility of the MRS fell into roughly equal groups of opponents (four), proponents (four), and skeptics or undecided (five). In the end, all voted to approve the report and said their concerns about safety had been resolved. Six months later, however, one initial opponent would now vote "no," largely because of recurring doubts about DOE's ability to fulfill its commitments to the TF.

All members expressed a considerable sense of pride and satisfaction about their TF participation and achievements and the personal commitment demonstrated by all. Each study group believed that its area of study and contribution was the most important. They believed that what they did as a TF would matter. Many were surprised at how much work was required and at the commitment of fellow members despite personal costs. Several mentioned their pride in having completed the large task and in making the necessary sacrifices in time, vacations, and lost pay.

This pride in the group accomplishment—as well as the expectations and comments of members—give evidence that the TF developed its own identity. Several members expect to be reconvened in the event that the MRS proposal is revived or approved by Congress. Three expressed concerns about the use of TF members by the city to lobby for the conditional MRS proposal after their report had been accepted by both local governmental bodies. Another was concerned that final negotiations by city and county might give up conditions without approval of TF members. A certain *esprit de corps* among members was evident months later.

EVALUATION AND CONCLUSIONS

We evaluate the pragmatic and creative record of the Clinch River MRS Task Force and responses to it in five parts: report content, group process within the TF, distrust of the developer (DOE), legitimacy and independence of the TF, and the lessons that can be drawn for local and NWPA siting processes.

Report Content

The TF report shows wide-ranging pragmatic concerns that this proposed federal nuclear waste facility not endanger people, the environment, or the social and economic structure. Conditions placed on the MRS siting sought to change the local net benefit balance from negative to positive. Using a creative, pragmatic approach, the TF conditions exemplify three major institutional perspectives of risk management (Rayner, 1984).

Examples of risk management conditions favored by market-oriented institutions include impact and full tax equivalency payments from time of authorization—not just construction—and opportunity costs for lost economic development potential of the MRS site. Hierarchically oriented risk management conditions include property value insurance for immediate neighbors of the MRS, compensation for the effects of negative perceptions of nuclear waste, and preventing the MRS from becoming a de facto permanent repository. Risk management conditions favored by egalitarian groups include a citizen oversight board with power to stop accepting waste under specified conditions, community environmental monitoring, and transportation safety mitigations.

The detailed concept of the citizen oversight board was considered by many TF members to be their greatest achievement. Incentives as well as mitigation and compensation were requested, with nonmonetary incentives receiving as much attention as economic ones. For another view of the MRS TF report as a successful multifaceted compensation plan, see Sigmon (1987).

After concluding that the technology for the MRS could be safe, the TF focused upon safety management and long-term assurances of proper operation rather than upon the safety of the technology *per se*. They sought to: (1) develop enduring mechanisms and institutions able to deal with uncertainty and flexible enough to adapt to new information and technologies, and (2) ensure an equitable course despite the vagaries of federal nuclear waste policy and the usual self-protective responses of large bureaucracies. It is not clear, however, that a citizen oversight board and local environmental monitoring mechanisms, even if agreed to by DOE, would be adequate for achieving their objectives. In restrospect, the NWPA amendments of 1987 show some limited response from Congress to TF appeals for help in arranging these and other guarantees.

Task Force Group Processes

The intensive questioning and group interaction processes within the TF were critical to developing trust and achieving consensus among members with different geographical and technical/nontechnical backgrounds. The safety decision as well as the development of conditions for acceptability were both made in this fashion. By their own report and researcher observations, interpersonal interaction and the group dynamic were more important than quantitative data or evaluation for reaching the safety decision.

Distrust of the Developer (DOE)

Dealing with distrust of DOE and other institutions was a principal objective of the TF, calling forth some of its most creative conditions. Recognizing their own doubts, skepticism, and suspicion of DOE, NRC, and the state, TF members saw the corrosive effects of this distrust as a key block to local acceptance of an MRS and as the principal reason for opposition. Like Hirschhorn (1984), they asked what could be done to rebuild trust and minimize distrust.

Thus were born their ideas about citizen input to the performance standards for the MRS, the citizen oversight board with authority to stop accepting waste if these standards were violated, and performance standards for DOE itself. Since DOE's past record of indifference to its pollution of the local environment was a main source of citizen distrust, the TF asked that the MRS construction schedule be linked to progress on DOE reservation cleanup.

Members considered that only concrete steps to create a better record of accountability could permit renewed trust by citizens in the MRS siting and operation. Although DOE saw its MRS operations as separate and independent, citizens did not. Positive interactions with the local MRS office were important in achieving negotiated conditions for acceptance, but a permanent change in DOE attitudes was seen as unlikely—and not enough to warrant citizen belief in DOE trustworthiness.

Safety management conditions asked by the TF went well beyond those required by NRC, the licensing agency. Nor did the TF entirely trust the state to provide the monitoring or administer the shutdown provisions it deemed necessary for long-term safety assurance. While opponents generally approved of TF conditions in private, they opposed the act of bargaining with DOE, saying they thought DOE would not or could not keep its end of the bargain, no matter what was in the formal agreement.

Legitimacy and Independence of the Task Force

Legitimacy of the MRS Clinch River Task Force was limited to the local area and DOE. Opponents attacked the TF and its report despite its inclusion of egalitarian conditions—such as local control and monitoring. In fact, one national opponent specifically opposed the local monitoring conditions. A partial reason for this opposition was the absence of environmental group representatives on any legitimate TF.

Other state and regional interests did not participate on the local TF or in similar groups with DOE. A local TF, no matter how competent and thorough, cannot speak for other areas and interests. While having technical insiders as members aided the TF by providing quick access to necessary expertise and information and helped legitimize the TF with DOE, their presence hindered TF legitimacy with the state and region. Most opponents, for instance, assumed that insiders dominated or contaminated the TF, making it a "DOE mouthpiece."

Questions about TF independence addressed by us included possible pressures from employers or local governments, internal pressures within a group bent upon consensus, implicit pressure from a pronuclear community, and effects of self-selection of Oak Ridge TF members. There was no evidence of employer pressures or interference by local government officials. Analysis of TF internal operations revealed considerable openness of approach and in-depth questioning of the adequacy of both the technology and management of a possible MRS, unlike the avoidance of difficult questions or protection of implicit group values that is characteristic of group think. Two of the three subgroup chairmen solicited minority votes on intermediate and final decisions to be certain that no differences were overlooked.

As might be expected, the TF represented local values. Its conclusions were clearly enabled by the supportive nuclear climate, but its extensive acceptance requirements went beyond any local base and reflect the independence of the TF analysis of safety and other needs.

Our data do not permit full evaluation of the effects of self-selection of the city's TF members, but interviews with all volunteers who were *not* selected by the city council show them to be very much like those who were chosen in occupation, opinions, and satisfaction with the TF report. Local antinuclear activists did not volunteer for the MRS TF.

Lessons Learned

Lessons drawn from this local effort to evaluate a proposed nuclear waste facility and negotiate conditions to make its siting acceptable were numerous. They include the items outlined in the following sections.

The Task Force and Its Operations

1. A citizen task force can be a successful mechanism for lay people (nonexperts) to evaluate information and reach a local consensus on safety and acceptability of a complex proposed facility. It is an alternative to the increasing but unsatisfactory reliance on advocacy science.

2. A citizen task force is an expensive method in terms of time, resources, and skills. It requires citizen commitment, intensive interaction, and staff support.

3. Developer—in this instance, DOE—funds were critical in enabling TF operation.

4. The intensive nature of TF operations was vital to the outcome. Consensus and group identity may not develop under less-demanding conditions.

Relationships and Negotiation with DOE

1. The informal negotiation process between DOE and the TF led to development of many conditions acceptable to both. The process is unfinished, however, with final outcome uncertain.

2. DOE deserves plaudits for its flexibility and responsiveness in dealing with local concerns in this instance.

3. The TF and city negotiated the nature of the TF's relationship with DOE as well as the specific conditions for a proposed siting.

4. TF conditions were aimed at changing the institutional relationship between DOE and local governments. (See also Sigmon, 1987.)

Siting Process and the Nuclear Waste Policy Act

1. Problems of distrust of the developer and federal agencies were addressed by (a) concrete measures aimed at demonstrating new, trustworthy performance and (b) interactive participation with the citizen task force in a problem-solving mode.

2. Standard socioeconomic analysis was largely irrelevant to the problems addressed by the TF, most of which were nonstandard assessment issues— such as management, accountability, and long-term assurances. In part, this is because the NWPA provides the framework for addressing many standard social impacts.

3. Local TF legitimacy can be enhanced by inclusion of interest group representatives, balanced technical/nontechnical and geographical composition, restraint in use of technical insiders as members, restriction of pro or con statements by authorities during its life, and avoiding use of the TF in a promotional role.

4. Negotiation and some level of trust are essential to enable citizens to consider the primary questions of safety. Decisions on acceptability are contingent upon decisions on safety.

5. Transferability of these findings may be limited by unique aspects of the Oak Ridge/Roane County area and its TF: a generally supportive local climate, familiarity with large federal nuclear projects, availability of in-house technical resources and expertise, and TF self-confidence in its own conclusions and in dealing with DOE. Transferable components may include the TF's conditional strategy, extra safety measures, some process components, and handling of distrust.

6. Interest by officials of a neighboring county in having the MRS with additional tailored conditions provided unexpected validation of TF success in creating a positive local net benefit balance.

7. More than local acceptance is required if the complex set of interests and actors in a nuclear waste facility siting is to be satisfied. In this case, while

local interests were dealt with satisfactorily, regional and state players never participated in a similar process of evaluation and negotiation. Negotiation did not fit the state strategy of opposition.

8. The 1987 changes to the Nuclear Waste Policy Act are a mixed bag in terms of responsiveness to host area concerns, but they do demonstrate a limited response to the MRS TF recommendations. For instance, they require that (a) the benefits package negotiation include consultation with affected local governments, (b) MRS benefits parallel those for the underground repository in most cases, (c) states transfer at least one-third of benefit payments to affected local governments, and (d) the Secretary of Energy's signature on a valid benefits agreement is a commitment by the U.S. government to make payments. In addition, local governments are given the right to appoint an on-site representative with oversight powers, paid by the Waste Fund. Unfortunately, the requirement that local and state governments waive their right to object to the siting or forfeit mitigation payments and a lump sum benefit complicates the negotiation process and may negate the advantages of the other changes in developing public acceptance of MRS siting arrangements. The amendments were highly responsive to TF concerns that the MRS would become a de facto permanent repository, adopting TF recommendations on tight linkage of MRS construction with repository licensing, and limiting of the quantity of spent fuel storage in an MRS to 10,000 tons prior to repository operation.

9. The NWPA needs revision to allow local negotiation and direct local contracts with DOE. Negotiation replaced adjudication in this application of NWPA (Sigmon, 1987) only in local aspects of siting.

10. The strongest message, however, is that much more attention must be given to local control and power-sharing measures if local acceptance of nuclear waste facilities is to be achieved. If Oak Ridge and Roane County, in an area long familiar with nuclear R&D activities and their management, set such conditions to overcome distrust, it is unlikely that any other locale will be satisfied with less.

This successful local exercise for arranging acceptable conditions for siting a generally unwanted facility is but one piece of a complex set of arrangements. Thus the MRS chapter raised more questions than it answered. The big questions cannot be answered by this study: Why did negotiation not occur between DOE and the state? Did DOE try hard enough to negotiate with state authorities? Why did DOE not negotiate the MRS site location as it did local site acceptance? The MRS experience did not meet the criterion that all stakeholders see some benefit from the siting (Cotton, 1986). How should DOE have structured its interaction with regional and state interest groups?

Likewise, the thorny problems of public participation in controversial public decision making in a democracy remain unsolved: How do we arrange for appropriate citizen input without permitting opponents to disrupt the proceedings and prevent decisions of which they disapprove? Would the statewide course of events have been different if the need for an MRS were more obvious? Finally, in the matter of public trust and distrust, how do we arrange to get on the road to "maybe" as did the Clinch River MRS Task Force rather than the polarized "yes-no" track followed by the Hartsville area and the rest of the state of Tennessee?

ACKNOWLEDGMENTS

Helpful comments and reviews of this chapter as it developed were given by colleagues in the Energy Division of Oak Ridge National Laboratory, including Steve Rayner, David Neal, Amy Wolfe, John H. Reed, Tom Wilbanks, and H. E. Zittel. The semifinal draft improved with editing by Amy Wolfe, while John Reed suggested and designed the illustration on MRS Task Force information sources. Reed's experience as a consultant and workshop leader for the MRS socioeconomic group made him a knowledgeable sounding board for many of the ideas developed herein.

Special thanks to the 13 task force members who shared thoughtful comments and insights from their TF experience in lengthy interviews, and who graciously tolerated my probing both into details and overall evaluations. Two of them, Shirley Hendrix and Charles Coutant, also reviewed drafts.

NOTES

1. Both EnvirG and SEG divided issues into standard and nonstandard impacts, devoting most effort to the latter. Standard impacts are those conventionally seen in the environmental impact literature, such as results of increased employment and worker transportation, effects upon community infrastructure and services—schools, roads, water, and sewer, for instance—including the need for growth management. Nonstandard impacts, usually less quantifiable, include impacts upon community social structure and long-term economic viability, distrust of the developer, and how to assure long-term accountability and safe management of the facility.

2. This deliberate process for achieving consensus was not recognized by the local press, which ridiculed "nitpicking" at this "boring meeting."

3. Sources for this section include 40 Tennessee newspapers for the period April 1985 through May 1986, particularly the Knoxville News-Sentinel, Knoxville Journal, The Tennessean (Nashville), Chattanooga Times, Chattanooga News-Free Press, Roane County News, Oak Ridger, Clinton Courier, Maryville Times, The Commercial Appeal (Memphis), and Jackson Sun.

BIBLIOGRAPHY

Armour, Audrey, ed. 1984. *Hazardous Waste Management: The "Not-in-My-Backyard" Syndrome*. Symposium Proceedings. May 13–14, 1983, Faculty of Environmental Studies. Downsview, Ontario: York University.

Bronfman, Ben. 1977. "A Study of Community Leaders in a Nuclear Host Community: Local Issues. Expectations and Support and Opposition." Report No. ORNL/TM–5997. Oak Ridge, Tenn.: Oak Ridge National Laboratory.

Carnes, Sam, E. Copenhaver, J. Sorensen, E. Soderstrom, J. H. Reed, D. Bjornstad, and E. Peelle. 1983. "Incentives and Nuclear Waste Siting: Prospects and Constraints." *Energy Systems and Policy* 7, no.4: 323–351.

Clinch River Monitored Retrievable Storage (MRS) Task Force. 1985. *Recommendations on the Proposed Monitored Retrievable Storage Facility*. Roane County and City of Oak Ridge, Tenn., October 15.

————. 1986. *MRS Submission to Congress*. Letter to Ben Rusche, Director of Office of Civilian Radioactive Waste Management, U.S. Department of Energy.

Colglazier, E. William. 1986. "The MRS: An Assessment of Its Need and Feasibility." *Forum for Applied Research and Public Policy*. 1, no. 1: 25–37.

Cotton, Thomas. 1986. "The MRS Facility: Radioactive Waste Management at a Crossroads." *Forum for Applied Research and Public Policy* 1, 1: 10–24.

Five County Research, Evaluation, Analysis and Liaison Group. 1985. "Recommendations on the Proposed Monitored Retrievable Storage Facility at the Hartsville TVA Nuclear Plant Site." Hartsville, Tenn.

Hirschhorn, Joel. 1984. "Siting Hazardous Waste Facilities." *Hazardous Waste* 1, no. 3: 423–429.

King, Joseph. 1986. "The DOE's MRS Proposal: Responding to Community Concerns." *Nuclear News* 29: 59–60.

Office of Technology Assessment. 1985. *Comments on Department of Energy's Mission Plan for the Civilian Radioactive Waste Management Program*. Washington, D.C.

O'Hare, Michael. 1977. "Not on My Block, You Don't: Facility Siting and the Strategic Importance of Compensation." *Public Policy* 25: 407–425.

O'Hare, Michael, L. Bacow, and D. Sanderson. 1983. *Facility Siting and Public Opposition*. New York: Van Nostrand and Reinhold.

Peelle, Elizabeth and Richard Ellis. 1986. "Beyond the 'Not-in-My-Backyard' Impasse." *Forum for Applied Research and Public Policy* 2, no. 3: 68–77.

Rayner, Steve. 1984. "Disagreeing About Risk: The Institutional Cultures of Risk Management and Planning for Future Generations." In *Risk Analysis, Institutions and Public Policy*, Susan Hadden, ed. New York: Associated Faculty Press, pp. 150–178.

Reed, John H. 1986. Private communication. Oak Ridge National Laboratory.

Sigmon, E. Brent. 1987. "Achieving a Negotiated Compensation Agreement in Siting: The MRS Case." *Journal of Policy Analysis and Management* 6, no. 2: 170–179.

Sorenson, John, J. Soderstrom, and S. Carnes. 1983. "Sweet for the Sour: Incentives in Environmental Mediation." *Environmental Management* 18: 287–294.

USA Today. 1986. (January 16).

U.S. Department of Energy. 1985a. Office of Civilian Radioactive Waste Management. *Monitored Retrievable Storage-Site Screening and Evaluation Process*. MRS–1.

————. 1985b. Office of Civilian Radioactive Waste Management. *The Role of the Monitored Retrievable Storage Facility in an Integrated Waste Management System*. MRS–3.

————. 1986. Office of Civilian Radioactive Waste Management. *MRS Submission to Congress, Environmental Assessment for a MRS*. Vol. 2, DOE/RW–0035–1, Rev. 1.

————. 1987. Office of Civilian Radioactive Waste Management. *Monitored Retrievable Storage Submission to Congress, Proposal for Construction of a MRS*. Vol. 1, DOE/RW–0035, Rev. 1.

Background Reading

Brubaker, Sterling, ed. 1984. *Rethinking the Federal Lands*. Washington, D.C.: Resources for the Future.

Carstensen, Vernon, ed. 1962. *The Public Lands: Studies in the History of the Public Domain*. Madison, WI: University of Wisconsin Press.

Clawson, Marion. 1972. *America's Land and Its Uses*. Baltimore: Johns Hopkins Press.

Clawson, Marion. 1983. *The Federal Lands Revisited*. Washington, D.C.: Resources for the Future.

————. 1975. *Forests for Whom and for What?* Baltimore: Johns Hopkins University Press.

————. 1971. *The Bureau of Land Management*. New York: Praeger.

Clawson, Marion, and Jack L. Knetsch. 1966. *Economics of Outdoor Recreation*. Baltimore: Johns Hopkins University Press.

Commission on Fair Market Value Policy for Federal Coal Leasing. 1984. *Report*. Washington, D.C.: Commission on Fair Market Value Policy for Federal Coal Leasing.

Council on Environmental Quality. 1985. *Fifteenth Annual Report of the Council on Environmental Quality*. Washington, D.C.: Government Printing Office. (Annual reports for other years are also valuable.)

Culhane, Paul J. 1981. *Public Lands Politics—Interest Group Influence on the Forest Service and the Bureau of Land Management*. Washington, D.C.: Resources for the Future.

Dana, Samuel T., and Sally K. Fairfax. 1980. *Forest and Range Policy*, 2d ed. New York: McGraw-Hill.

Everhart, William C. 1972. *National Park Service*. New York: Praeger.

Fitch, James Marston. 1982. *Historic Preservation: Curatorial Management of the Built Environment*. New York: McGraw-Hill.

Foresta, Ronald A. 1985. *America's National Parks and Their Keepers*. Washington, D.C.: Resources for the Future.

Foss, Phillip. 1960. *Politics and Grass*. Seattle: University of Washington Press.

Fradkin, Philip L. 1984. *A River No More: The Colorado River and the West*. Tucson, AZ: University of Arizona Press.

Gates, Paul W. 1968. *History of Public Land Law Development*. Washington, D.C.: Government Printing Office.

Grey, G. W., and F. J. Deneke. 1978. *Urban Foresty*. New York: John Wiley and Sons.

Hall, C. A. S., and John W. Day, Jr. 1977. *Ecosystem Modeling in Theory and in Practice*. New York: John Wiley and Sons.

Hays, Samuel P. 1959. *Conservation and the Gospel of Efficiency*. Cambridge, MA: Harvard University Press.

Howe, Charles W. 1979. *Natural Resource Economics: Issues, Analysis, and Policy*. New York: John Wiley and Sons.

Ise, John. 1962. *Our National Park Policy—A Critical History*. Baltimore: Johns Hopkins Press.

Johnston. George M., and Peter M. Emerson, eds. 1984. *Public Lands and the U.S. Economy—Balancing Conservation and Development*. Boulder, CO: Westview Press.

LeMaster, Dennis C. 1984. *Decade of Change: The Remaking of Forest Service Statutory Authority During the 1970s*. Westport, Conn.: Greenwood Press.

Leshy, John D. 1987. *The Mining Law: A Study in Perpetual Motion*. Washington. D.C.: Resources for the Future.

Manks, J. B. et al. 1984. *Dispute Resolution in America: Process in Evolution*. Washington. D.C.: National Institute for Dispute Resolution.

Nash, Roderick. 1973. *Wilderness and the American Mind*, rev. ed. New Haven, CT: Yale University Press.

Nelson, Robert H. 1983. *The Making of Federal Coal Policy*. Durham, NC: Duke University Press.

Odum, E. P. 1971. *Fundamentals of Ecology*, 3d ed. Philadelphia: W. B. Saunders Press.

Patric, William C, 1981. *Trust Land Administration in the Western States*. Denver: Public Lands Institute.

Pneuman, R. W., and M. E. Bruehl. 1982, *Managing Conflict* Englewood Cliffs, NJ: Prentice-Hall.

Public Land Law Review Commission. 1970. *One Third of the Nation's Land*. Washington, D.C.: Government Printing Office.

Raiffa, Howard. 1982. *The Art and Science of Negotiations*. Cambridge, MA: Harvard University Press.

Robinson. Glen O. 1975. *The Forest Sevice—A Study in Public Land Management*. Baltimore: Johns Hopkins University Press.

Sax, Joseph L. 1980. *Mountains Without Handrails: Reflections on the National Parks*. Ann Arbor, MI: University of Michigan Press.

Shands, William E., 1979. *Federal Resource Land and Their Neighbors*. Washington. D.C.: Conservation Foundation.

Shands, William E., and Robert G. Healy. 1977. *The Lands Nobody Wanted*. Washington D.C.: Conservation Foundation.

Steen, Harold K. 1976. *The U.S. Forest Service: A History.* Seattle: University of Washington Press.

Truluck, Phillip N., ed. 1983. *Private Rights and Public Lands.* Washington. D.C.: The Heritage Foundation.

Voight, William, Jr. 1976. *Public Grazing Lands: Use and Misuse by Industry and Government.* New Brunswick, NJ: Rutgers University Press.

Wehr, Paul. 1979. *Conflict Regulation.* Boulder, CO: Westview Press.

Wolf, Peter. 1981. *Land in America: Its Value, Use and Control.* New York: Pantheon Books.

Wyant, William K. 1982. *Westward in Eden.* Berkeley, CA: University of California Press.

Index

About the Contributors

NORMAN A. BERG, Chief of the Soil Conservation Service from 1979 to 1982, is now senior advisor with American Farmland Trust. He was the recipient in 1973 of the USDA Distinguished Service Award, and in 1980 of the National Wildlife Federation's Conservation Achievement Award.

JOSEPH B. BROWDER is a consultant to industry on conflict management, resource development, regulation, and legislation. He was an official in the U.S. Interior Department from 1977 to 1980, cofounder of the Environmental Policy Institute, former Conservation Director of Friends of the Earth, and southeastern representative of the National Audubon Society.

MARION CLAWSON is senior fellow emeritus of Resources for the Future in Washington, D.C. He has been associated with Resources for the Future in various capacities since 1955, including directorship of the land and water studies program as well as vice president and acting president. Earlier in his distinguished career, he worked in the U.S. Department of Agriculture's Bureau of Economics and later served as director of the Bureau of Land Management in the Department of the Interior. Over a period of several decades, he has authored a number of authoritative books in the area of public lands and land-use management. In 1988 he received the National Wildlife Federation's Conservation Achievement Award.

PIERRE CROSSON is a senior fellow at Resources for the Future, where he has been since 1965. His Ph.D. in economics is from Columbia University. His research has long been focused on the management of agricultural land and its long-term consequences for production and environmental values.

JACK DOYLE is Director of Agricultural Resources Project and has been with Environmental Policy Institute since 1974. He is the author of *Altered Harvests* (1985), and recently testified before a congressional committee on release of genetically altered organisms into the environment.

BENJAMIN C. DYSART III is a past president of National Wildlife Federation, a trustee of the René Dubos Center, a senior fellow of The Conservation Foundation, member of the EPA Science Advisory Board, U.S. Army Chief of Engineer's Environmental Advisory Board, Electric Power Research Institute's Advisory Council, a former member of the U.S. Department of the Interior's Outer Continental Shelf Advisory Board and its scientific committee, a member of the National Park Service's Glacier National Park Science Council, and a professor of environmental and water resources engineering at Clemson University. He teaches graduate courses in resources planning and environmental protection, is a consultant to corporations and agencies in these areas, conducts research on linkages among components in land and water resources systems, and was general chairman of the René Dubos Center's Forum on Land Use Management.

RAYMOND C. LOEHR holds the Hussein M. Alharthy Centennial Chair in civil engineering at the University of Texas, Austin. His activities encompass teaching, research, and advising to regulatory agencies, industries, and consulting firms. He serves as chairman of the Executive Committee of the U.S. Environmental Protection Agency's Science Advisory Board. His professional interests include industrial and hazardous waste management, especially multimedia aspects.

DAVID L. MORELL is Vice President-Environmental Affairs of Ensco Environmental Services, Inc., Fremont, California. He is a specialist on facility siting and permitting, and on innovative solutions to hazardous waste management problems. His career includes experience in senior positions with the U.S. Environmental Protection Agency in both Washington, D.C. and San Francisco, and as toxics coordinator for Santa Clara County, California. He teaches part time in Stanford University's Department of Environmental Engineering and has authored or co-authored numerous publications, including *Siting Hazardous Waste Facilities: Local Opposition and the Myth of Preemption* (1982) and "The Elusive Pursuit of Toxics Management" (1988).

ELIZABETH PEELLE is an Environmental Sociologist in the Technology and Social Systems Group, Energy Division, Oak Ridge National Laboratory. She helped develop the field of social impact assessment for the U.S. government. She works on equitable institutional arrangements for host areas in siting nuclear/hazardous waste facilities.

R. NEIL SAMPSON is Executive Vice President of the American Forestry Association in Washington, D.C. He formerly served in the same capacity for the National Association of Conservation Districts. Earlier in his career, he served in many jobs with the U.S. Soil Conservation Service. He has written and lectured extensively on a wide variety of conservation and resource policy topics, and regularly serves as a consultant to congressional committees considering natural resource legislation. He has served on the Board of Directors of the American Land Forum and the National Nonpoint Source Institute.

JOHN A. THORNER served as Environmental Counsel and Director of Communications for the American Paper Institute and the National Forest Products Association's Environmental and Health Program in Washington, D.C., until December 1987. There he was responsible for managing air quality and forest health issues. Currently, he is serving as Director of Government Affairs and General Counsel for the Water Pollution Control Federation, which is based in Alexandria, Virginia.

EVAN C. VLACHOS is a professor of sociology and civil engineering at Colorado State University. He is a former Director of the Environmental Resources Center. He has acted as consultant on a variety of environmental projects. From 1982 to 1987 he served as Chairman of the Environmental Advisory Board, U.S. Army Corps of Engineers.